SAMUEL PARTIDA, JR.

The Illinois Impeachment & Prior Inconsistent Statement Handbook

First published by IllinoisCaseLaw.com 2019

Copyright © 2019 by Samuel Partida, Jr.

All rights reserved. No part of this publication may be reproduced, stored or transmitted in any form or by any means, electronic, mechanical, photocopying, recording, scanning, or otherwise without written permission from the publisher. It is illegal to copy this book, post it to a website, or distribute it by any other means without permission.

Consuming the content on this book does not constitute legal advice nor establish an attorney-client relationship. The information is intended for general education and informational purposes only. The information herein should not be interpreted to indicate a certain result will occur in your specific legal situation. Every case is unique and different. Specific outcomes are dependent on the particular circumstances of each case.

Although reasonable efforts are made to present the most recent information, you should not assume that the information provided herein is the most recent. Nor should you assume that the information is in your best interest. Consuming the information in this book should never be a substitute for advice and representation from a qualified, duly licensed attorney in your jurisdiction.

Although I personally limit my practice to the criminal law. The Supreme Court of Illinois does not recognize certifications of specialties in the practice of law, nor does it recognize certifications of expertise in any phase of the practice of law by any agency, governmental or private, or by any group, organization or association.

First edition

ISBN: 9781986174633

This book was professionally typeset on Reedsy.
Find out more at reedsy.com

Contents

Introduction & A Quote You Must Read	1
Why Do We Keep Screwing This Up?	6
What Is Impeachment?	11
Impeachment v. Substantive Evidence	17
Marlo, Omar, & Betty (A Small Example)	19
How To Classically Impeach A Witness	23
The 3 C's (The Basics)	24
The 3 C's (Deeper Dive)	25
The Impeaching Witness	36
Affirmative Damage Rule	37
Good-Faith Basis	43
Final Thoughts	46
The Statute & The Rules of Evidence	48
The Elements Of A Prior Inconsistent Statement	62
Just Like Classical Impeachment	62
Threshold Issues	64
Bar Shooting In The Early Morning Example	65
The Personal Knowledge Requirement	74
What Defense Attorneys Should Know	75
The Acknowledgment Hearing	81
Unique To Illinois	81
A Domestic Violence Example	82
But Do I Have To?	85

The Danger Is Real	88
Judges Too	90
57 Pages And Five Examples Of "How To Do It"	95
The Reckless Homicide Impeaching Witness Example	95
The Granny Acknowledgment Hearing Example	101
My Brother Didn't Do It Example	111
Prosecutor Completely Loses Control Example	129
How To Think Through A Problem	145
The Checklist Bringing It All Together	153
About the Author	159

1

Introduction & A Quote You Must Read

It's rare to read something like this in a criminal law opinion:

> "More than 15 years after the General Assembly enacted the statute, the author of this opinion noted that 'even experienced trial courts face serious uncertainties when applying section 115-10.1 of the Code.' People v. Edwards, 309 Ill. App. 3d 447, 457, 722 N.E.2d 258, 265 (1999) (Steigmann, J., specially concurring). Now, more than 30 years after the statute's enactment, seasoned attorneys and trial judges still regularly mishandle section 115-10.1 issues when they come up at trial. To help clear up the confusion about the appropriate use of section 115-10.1(c)(2)(B) of the Code, which addresses a witness's acknowledgement of her prior inconsistent statement, we provide the following detailed explanation regarding the proper procedure to be followed under subsection (c)(2)(B)."

People v. Brothers, 2015 IL App (4th) 130644 (September), ¶ 66.

The judge is right.

You can debate whether it's a good idea to call out the entire Illinois trial bar, but there's no debating that mistakes in this area of the law are one of the most common trial errors occurring in Illinois courtrooms.

Any close tracking of published court opinions will quickly reveal case after case where trial attorneys stumble when they encounter a prior inconsistent statement. It's not just the trial attorneys either. Mistakes are happening at all levels, including judges.

This book is for trial attorneys. The goal of this book is to help clear up the confusion. If you do any amount of trial work you can bet this issue will come up again and again. This book is for anyone who has a desire to try cases in an Illinois criminal courtroom. If you want a trial without impeachment and prior inconsistent statement error this book is for you.

This small book is not intended to be a comprehensive "how to" on conducting proper cross-examination. Nor is it intended to be a comprehensive treatise on all evidentiary matters. You won't learn much more than how to properly deal with a testifying witness who has made a prior inconsistent statement. That's it. After reading this book you will, on the other hand, know exactly what to do (and what not to do) when you encounter a witness you know for a fact has made a different statement in the past.

INTRODUCTION & A QUOTE YOU MUST READ

Nothing more is promised nor explored in these pages. This book is all about learning how to conduct proper impeachment by prior inconsistent statement. Nothing more is aspired to nor intended in these pages.

In **Chapter 2** we'll explore some of the reasons why I think we keep seeing errors with this issue. There is no statistical analysis or anything like that. This is not that type of book.

In **Chapter 3** we'll answer what we mean when we use the term "impeachment." What does it mean exactly? We'll clear up some confusion around the word and other terms we use around this topic.

In **Chapter 4** we'll discuss the "old way" of doing things. You can also call this the rules under the "common law." I'm not a legal historian. I'm not referring to any specific time period or dates. We make a simple effort to understand what problems and solutions courts of law had before they wrote the current rules. For purposes of this book, I use the term "classical impeachment" to talk about the "old way" of doing things.

In **Chapter 5** we get into the nitty gritty on the issue. If you just want to know "how to impeach" a witness, you can flip to this chapter and beyond, but I'd caution about jumping too far ahead too soon. Many of the natural questions you may have in the later chapters are likely answered in the earlier chapters.

In **Chapter 6** we lay out the current relevant Illinois Rules of Evidence and the one important statute that lays out the law around impeachment and prior inconsistent statements. I threw in the Federal Rules of Evidence as well, but that was an afterthought.

In **Chapter 7** we analyze 725 ILCS 5/115-10.1. There are some practical examples in this chapter that walk you through how to use the statue to impeach a witness with a prior inconsistent statement.

In **Chapter 8** we address the acknowledgment hearing. This is something that, as far as I know, is unique to Illinois criminal law. Many attorneys are unaware of it, and if they are, it remains underutilized in criminal courtrooms.

In **Chapter 9** we'll look at 5 different case studies or examples of applying the principles from the earlier chapters. A few of these were inspired by actual cases. One fact pattern was lifted right out of a court opinion. In between the lines of questions and answers you'll find helpful and illuminating comments.

In **Chapter 10** we present some helpful resources and descriptions of where you can find additional resources on this topic. You'll also see a convenient checklist cheat sheet that you can copy and download for your trial binder.

I don't doubt you have your wits about you, and maybe you have a few good years and even some decades of trial experience under your belt. However, *knowing* something and *properly executing* under pressure appear to be two different things. If you are an experienced trial attorney I only ask that you humor me a bit and read through the book with a fresh mind.

INTRODUCTION & A QUOTE YOU MUST READ

I believe if you can momentarily forget what you know and come at this book with a clean slate you will pull out of it valuable information that may not currently be a part of your practice. If you are just beginning to experiment with mock trials or just dipping your toe into a trial courtroom, I promise you this book will not be *too advanced* for you.

I purposely kept the citations and the law-talk to a minimum. If you are just beginning to do trial work, this book is perfect for you because you'll begin to develop the habits that prevent you from being called out for committing the mistakes outlined in these pages.

Well then, now that that's out of the way. Onward to Chapter 2 where we ask and answer the question:

> *"Why do we keep screwing up impeachment and prior inconsistent statements during a trial?"*

2

Why Do We Keep Screwing This Up?

So what's going on?

Why do we keep making the same mistake at trial?

Judge Steigmann has been quoted as saying this is really "simple stuff." See bonus interview in Chapter 10. The modern rules are written down. They are right there on paper in black and white for any trial attorney to read and understand. On the other hand, there is quite a gap between "knowing what to do" and "properly executing" when the moment presents itself.

If there is just a little bit of confusion or misunderstanding around this topic, a trial is the last place to iron out the kinks. It's likely that many of the examples of error in the record are instances where the attorney immediately after the trial understood they flubbed the issue. It's no different than observing an athlete on the field shake their head in disappointment immediately after dropping the ball. They know how to catch a ball.

Yet it happens. Under the pressure of a game when the opposition is knocking you around balls get dropped. It's the same in a criminal trial. Even the smartest and most experienced among us are vulnerable to being knocked off our game in the middle of a heated trial. Under pressure, mistakes happen. That's trial work for you.

Trials move quickly. If an attorney has not sketched out an action plan or prepared some kind of response to the exact inconsistent statement that materializes during a trial, that's a circumstance that has a good chance of being recorded as error in the record.

The responsibility of an attorney is to "object" when they hear something objectionable. Counsel must instantly react with very little time to think. The attorney's reaction has to be quick and fast. There's a lot going on in the attorney's head in those precious seconds after a witness begins to go in a direction other than expected.

Additionally, troublesome witnesses are usually encountered on cross-examination. Cross is much different than direct-examination. On direct, the flow of the witness' testimony is more in the control of the attorney. Cross can sometimes feel like riding a bull that is beginning to buck. You know your job is to stay on the bull. You know if you stay on, you won't be gorged by the bull. Knowing what you have to do and doing it are two different things.

Then again, sometimes on direct it can also feel like a witness has just punched you in the face. The point is that it doesn't matter how "smart" you are. Staying calm and collected under trial pressure is something else.

The time that you have to stand up and object or react to a troublesome witness is unimaginably short. This is where true and tested "trial reflexes" have to kick in because you're not exactly going to get a chance to brief the issue. Stuff is going to fly right by you before you realize that you should have done something. This is what I suspect is happening with impeachment and prior inconsistent statement trial error.

There's no doubt about it. Impeachment by prior inconsistent statement comes up frequently in a criminal trial. In many ways the essence of a criminal trial is all about learning to deal with witnesses who are not testifying the way you thought they would. This concept is so fundamental to a criminal trial there's no getting around it. There's absolutely no avoiding it.

An attorney who hasn't built up their "impeachment reflex" will have their number come up eventually. The goal of this book is to minimize, maybe even zero out, the likelihood that you make a mistake when you are confronted with this issue during trial.

There are no hidden secrets. There is nothing unique, fundamental, or special that helps explain what's happening. We have a numbers game here.

This issue comes up frequently enough that it's overrepresented in the trial record. That means even attorneys with the best track record on this issue eventually catch a case where their guard is down. Eventually you will have a witness testify to something different than you expected.

You'll be caught off guard. That's exactly when a fumble happens. That's when the trial transcripts likely register "an error." The error gets sent up to the Appellate Court. An opinion is released, and we all get to read about it. This is how we keep adding case after case to the pile of cases marked with "impeachment error." The stumble doesn't mean the attorney is confused or misunderstands the issue. The attorney's number just came up.

The goal then is to build up your "impeachment reflex." We'll start at the beginning and build from there. You can flip to Chapter 10 to see the end result. There you'll find a checklist or cheat sheet of sorts, but if you take the time to process the chapters between here and there, you'll be better off.

The goal is not just to throw a few pointers your way. The goal is for you to internalize the ideas such that you own them. Once you understand the issues, you'll be in a far stronger position to start building your "reflex." The point is to get this reaction to the forefront of your mind, so you are doing minimal actual thinking during a trial. This is truly how you zero out impeachment errors. It takes a little brain power now so you don't have to think much during trial.

The hard work of understanding has to be done way before trial. This has to become a rote procedure. It has to be "built-in" and "instantaneous." You have to learn to react fast and reliably, so you can move on with the rest of the trial.

So let's begin with our choice of words. Part of the problem is that there is genuine confusion about the terminology. We're using the same words to stand for different things. That's a problem. Our first step is to get clear on what we mean by the term "impeachment."

3

What Is Impeachment?

- What does it mean to say a witness has been impeached?

- What is a prior inconsistent statement?

- What does it mean to be impeached with a prior inconsistent statement?

- What does it mean to have only impeachment value?

- What does it mean for a statement to have substantive evidence?

Imagine yourself in the middle of an active criminal trial. There's a prosecutor and a defense attorney. The prosecution begins by presenting their case with evidence that furthers their cause. The job of the defense is to undo and erase every bit of evidence raised by the prosecution. If the defense decides to put on a case, the same thing happens in reverse.

This is the essence of a criminal trial. Each side promotes their competing interests at the expense of the other side. This is an old-fashioned adversarial system.

In its broadest form, "impeachment" means to cancel out, minimize, or erase the other side's witness testimony as much as possible. This is a broad category that encompasses many things. But before moving on, let me emphasize this last point because it's important and worth mentioning again.

Impeachment means cancelling a witness's testimony.

That's it. There's nothing fancy here. Like I was saying, impeachment is a very broad subject. It can encompass various forms. Cross-examination itself is complex in large part because there are various forms of impeachment with which to attack a witness.

Witnesses can be impeached because they have a bad memory. Witness testimony can be cancelled if the witness is too emotionally attached to a party in the case. This is an emotional bias. There can be financial and professional bias that can be highlighted for the jury.

An eyewitness can be left on the stand unworthy of belief if you illustrate they had a bad viewing angle, it was too dark, or they didn't have their glasses with them. Too many serious felony convictions can leave a witness looking like a criminal and therefore discredited. There are all kinds of ways and manners to impeach witnesses and cancel their testimony.

Within this broad definition of impeachment, we will zero in on one, and only one, specific form. We are interested in impeachment of a witness by use of a prior inconsistent statement. That's when you cancel out a person's testimony by pointing out to the jury that this person has said something different in the past.

From this point forward, in this book, when you read the word "impeachment," it's being used the way I just described. In the real world, when you hear the term you'll have to clarify to make sure you understand how the term is being used. I think there are a lot of attorneys who only know "impeach" to mean confrontation in court with a prior inconsistent statement. From now on that is how we will use the term, but if you hear the word being used in a different way it's probably because the word is being used in the broader sense.

I like to think of impeachment with a prior inconsistent statement as "classical impeachment." All I mean by "classical impeachment" is that this is what they did before they wrote down the law on this topic. This isn't exactly a term of art in the business. If you want to picture a bunch of lawyers and judges in wigs, that's fine too.

I just want to make sure we take a small moment to travel back in time to understand what a criminal court was like before they figured everything out and wrote some rules down. I don't want to get too technical, but I guess I'm using the term "classical impeachment" to describe what happened during the common law when a witness was caught saying something different on the stand that they had said in the past.

Go back to the imaginary criminal trial going on in your head. Imagine all the attorneys have wigs on, so you know we are in the distant past. We are in the common law era, and none of the modern rules or laws on impeachment with a prior inconsistent statement have been formally written down yet.

In this world, impeachment by a prior inconsistent statement caused a very unique problem for the court. Two competing interests suddenly collided head-on. On the one hand, judges completely mistrusted any statement that occurred outside of the criminal proceeding. (To a large extent, courts still mistrust these statements, but there are now accepted exceptions for allowing into evidence some of them.)

Before the hearsay rules were hammered out, judges just assumed to keep those statements out of court. They were treated like the black death, a plague that was to be avoided. Any statement that was made outside the formal sanctity of the criminal courtroom was mistrusted.

On the other hand, that rule against hearsay statements butted heads directly with the truth-seeking function of a trial. There were plenty of instances, usually on cross, when a party knew for darn sure that a witness had said something different in the past. These attorneys were dying to confront witnesses with that prior inconsistent statement. Talk about an opportunity to impeach a witness.

Shoving a prior inconsistent statement in a witness's face is a great way to demonstrate to the jury that this witness can't be believed. On top of that, the out-of-court statement was often the more reliable statement. Nonetheless, if the hearsay rule was going to be strictly enforced, it meant an attorney on cross-examination would be left accepting the cockamamy-bull story regurgitated by the witness on the stand.

What to do? What to do, indeed.

Even though a person was known to have said something inconsistent, the out-of-court statement was hearsay and treated like trash by the court. All the reasons for disapproving of hearsay were front and center and had to be dealt with whenever an attorney wanted to impeach a witness with a prior inconsistent statement.

Particularly bothersome was the fact that the opposing party did not have the opportunity to effectively cross-examine the witness. Since the statement was made outside of court, opposing counsel couldn't be there to challenge the statement when the statement was made.

See the dilemma?

The fundamental problem for the court was what to do with those pesky prior inconsistent statements. Of course they wanted the trial process to serve as a truth-seeking mechanism. On the other hand, out-of-court statements were generally considered untested and unproven. Completely excluding the prior statement also didn't sit well with judges. That would mean allowing a witness to go unchallenged when opposing counsel could prove the witness said something different in the past.

The struggle between admitting a prior statement and hearsay rules is what "classical impeachment" was designed to address. In the next few pages we'll look at the solution they came up with for dealing with "classical impeachment."

4

Impeachment v. Substantive Evidence

In a world before the modern rules of evidence, what was a court to do with a witness who had completely changed their story?

Does the court allow the witness' story to go unchallenged, completely subverting the truth-seeking function of the court or does it allow the impeaching attorney to admit a prior inconsistent statement that was generally inadmissible?

Here's the rule they came up with:

> *Classical impeachment meant a witness could be confronted with a prior statement that conflicted with their in-court testimony, but the jury was instructed they could only consider the prior statement to judge the witness' veracity. In other words, the trier of fact was not allowed to use that statement as substantive evidence.*

So what does this mean?

The court was trying to balance these two competing interests. The balance was resolved by simply telling the impeaching party,

> *"I'm going to allow you to confront this witness with the prior out-of-court statement, however, you can only use it to impeach the witness, and you cannot argue the substance of the prior statement."*

In other words, you are allowed to use the prior statement to argue to the jury that they should not believe the witness' testimony given in court because that witness has said something different and is therefore unreliable. But that is all you are allowed to do.

You absolutely can not argue to the jury what the witness said in the prior statement is the truth. You are not allowed to tell them they should consider the witness' prior statement as proof that the statement is, in fact, true.

The prior inconsistent statement is not considered *real* evidence. The judge will tell the impeaching party to not even try to convince the jury that the the substance of the out-of-court statement is the truth. "Don't go there counselor," and things to that effect is the verbal warning an impeaching lawyer might hear.

It's a fine line the attorney had to walk. It was an even finer distinction the jury was being asked to make. Nonetheless, this is what the classical rule had become. It's actually pretty logical if you stop and think about it. If courts are naturally leery of out-of-court statements and simultaneously want to promote truth seeking, this compromise rule is exactly the way things would turn out. It is the most direct way of balancing the competing interests. One side gets to argue that the witness is a lying swine. The other side is protected by not allowing the prior statement to be used as substantive evidence.

Marlo, Omar, & Betty (A Small Example)

To see what they meant by "impeachment only" and not "substantive evidence," let's consider an easy example.

For instance, say we have a murder trial. A man has been shot and is lying in a parking lot bleeding. The police respond to the parking lot of a bar where shots were reported. Let's say that shortly after the shooting, the scene was chaotic. Say the defendant's best friend, Marlo, was not exactly aware of everything that was going on.

When Marlo comes out of the bar to the parking lot, he sees paramedics treating a guy on the ground. When an officer approaches Marlo, he asks him if he saw anything or if he knows the victim. Marlo is looking right at the guy on the ground. Marlos says to the officer,

"Not really. It's nobody I know. It's just some guy my homie, Omar, whooped-up for rapping on his girl, Betty."

After a long investigation, the police charge Marlo's best buddy, Omar, with the murder. Other witnesses say the dispute was over a girl inside the bar. By the time the trial comes along, Marlo realizes his best friend, Omar, is in a lot of trouble.

When the prosecution calls Marlo to the stand, Marlo is asked basic questions like how he knows the defendant and where he was the night of the shooting. Those questions go off without a hitch. Then the prosecution asks Marlo,

Q: "Did Omar get into an altercation with anyone at the bar that night?"

Marlo answers,

A: "Nah man, there was no trouble. Omar didn't get into it with nobody."

Obviously, the prosecutor is fuming. The prosecutor knows for a fact that Marlo told the police the guy who got shot was "whooped" by his buddy Omar earlier in the night inside the bar because the guy was rapping on Betty. Under the classical rules, the prosecution doesn't just have to accept Marlo's trial testimony. The prosecution is allowed to let the jury know that at the scene of the shooting Marlo said something very different.

Eventually, the jury hears that Omar told an officer,

"Not really. It's nobody I know. It's just some guy my homie, Omar, whooped-up for rapping on his girl, Betty."

The prosecution is warned to only use this statement for impeachment purposes. The judge makes it quite clear that the statement has no substantive value. The prosecution would have loved to argue to the jury that Marlo's statement to the officer at the scene of the shooting was proof that Omar got into an argument with the victim over his girlfriend Betty.

But the prosecution cannot do that. The prosecutor can only use the statement Marlo made to the police shortly after the shooting to argue to the jury that Marlo's court testimony cannot be believed. That's it. Nothing more. That's the only way the prosecution can use the earlier statement. The prior statement can only be used to cancel out Marlo's in-court testimony.

This is what it means to say that a party can only use a prior statement for purposes of impeachment while not at all using the statement substantively.

The classical rules of impeachment also evolved a specific procedure that had to be followed for impeachment with a prior inconsistent statement. The procedure has become as important as the rule itself. If a witness was not confronted with their prior inconsistent statement in the right way, the other side could make a "foundation" objection and keep the whole statement out. In turn, this special "foundation" procedure exists to make sure that not too much information is elicited about a prior inconsistent statement.

From the court's perspective, allowing the jury to hear any of the prior statement was bad enough. The court certainly wasn't going to make it easy to get into any other broader statements. Remember, under classical impeachment there is a danger of allowing too much "untested" information before the jury.

This impeachment versus substantive evidence dichotomy remains viable to the present day. This is a concept that has survived into modern criminal courtrooms. Any trial attorney today still has to be able to quickly tell the difference between a prior statement being used for impeachment only and a prior statement that might be allowed for substantive evidence. We don't want to get ahead of ourselves just yet. Soon we'll talk more about prior statements that can be used as substantive evidence.

Let's first make sure we understand the "foundation" requirement an attorney has to follow when they impeach a witness with a prior inconsistent statement. You may have heard of the "3 C's" for impeachment or maybe the "RAC system" for impeachment. Both of these deal with the three foundational elements that always have to be present for proper classical impeachment.

5

How To Classically Impeach A Witness

Here we discuss the mechanics of how to conduct proper impeachment. The way it is done matters.

This specific procedure was developed to help alleviate some of the concerns discussed earlier. There is a "right way" to impeach a witness and a "wrong way." Anything not done the right way is the wrong way. You have to do it this way, or you aren't allowed to do it at all. It's that simple.

These preliminary steps are also called the "foundation" for proper impeachment.

Some trial instructors call this the RAC (pronounced "rack") system for proper impeachment. I prefer the 3 C's (CCC) version of the rule. The name doesn't matter. The same three steps always have to be followed before a lawyer is allowed to impeach a witness with a prior statement.

The acronym under the RAC system stands for the following:

- Re-Commit
- Accredit
- Confront

In the 3 C's system, the C's stand for the following:
- Commit
- Confirm
- Confront

The name doesn't matter, the only thing that is important is that these three foundation steps be followed.

The 3 C's (The Basics)

First C (Commit) - To start this process it's very important to give the witness a chance to testify consistently with the prior statement. At the first hint that the witness is saying something different from the earlier statement, you have to give the witness a chance to clarify or to commit to their statement.

Second C (Confirm) - In the second step, you need to confirm the time, place, location, and circumstances of the prior statement for the witness. This part feels more like traditional foundation-type questions where you are familiarizing the witness with the details of the original statement.

Third C (Confront) - Only after these foundational steps are followed can you finally confront the witness with the prior inconsistent statement. But even this has to be done in a certain way.

The 3 C's (Deeper Dive)

Learning to impeach a witness with the 3 C's remains alive and relevant in today's courtroom. We are still following the 3 C's. This is still the same procedure used to properly impeach a witness with a prior inconsistent statement. We'll now take an even deeper dive into how one should use the 3 C's to impeach a witness.

First C (Commit) - You can think of the first step as a chance for the witness to commit to their inconsistent statement. You're basically giving them a chance to get it right. It's up to them, but you have to give them the chance.

The best way I've seen to do this is by asking the question the way you would have preferred it be answered rather than simply re-asking what the witness said. You give the witness a chance to get it "right" by saying it "right" for them. At this point the witness can either go in the direction you have set for them or they can stick to their inconsistent testimony.

For example, think back to the Marlo example. Marlo was called to testify against his friend accused of murder. The prosecution thought Marlo was going to testify about a fight the defendant had gotten into earlier that night in the bar with the victim.

Instead, at trial Marlo said,

"Nah man, there was no trouble. Omar didn't get into it with nobody."

The prosecution could establish the first C simply by asking,

Q: "Are you saying Omar didn't get into a fight with the victim earlier in the night at the bar?"

Now Marlo has a choice to either commit to this testimony or he can take the opportunity to testify consistently with the prior statement he made to police at the scene of the shooting.

The other way for the prosecution to do it is by phrasing the "committal" question in terms favorable to the state. The prosecutor could have asked,

Q: "Are you saying Omar *DID* get into a fight with the victim?"

Marlo still has the same choice to make after this question. He can commit to his trial testimony or he can testify consistently with the out-of-court statement. It's up to him.

Second C (Confirm) - When you confirm the statement you essentially go through the circumstances of the statement. The bare minimum is to make sure you cover the time (date and time of day), place (address or location), and other people present for the statement. At this point, all you are doing is getting the witness ready for the final step. A lot of attorneys get caught up here when the witness refuses to confirm the information.

If that happens you just keep going.

All you are doing is putting the witness on notice as to what is coming. The witness doesn't have to, strictly speaking, confirm these details. It's just your job to give the witness a chance to get on the same page. The point of the second C is to lay out the details around the making of the statement. That's it.

Even here, there is room for experienced attorneys to be persuasive. Experienced counsel just don't settle for the minimum. They really ham-up this element. It's the jury more than the witness who needs to know the details of the statement. If the jury knows these details, it will be easier for them to conclude that the witness was more credible at the time of the prior statement.

Let's look at a domestic violence example. In this case, the victim told the officer who responded to her home that her boyfriend slapped and punched her. The boyfriend is arrested and charged with domestic battery.

At the trial, girlfriend gets on the stand and says that she hurt herself on accident. As soon as she utters those words, she has to be asked the initial commitment question to give her a chance to get it right.

Q: "Did you say, your boyfriend *HURT* you?"

A: "No. It was an accident. I hurt myself."

At this point, you get right into the time, place, and circumstance of the statement (2nd C—confirm).

Q: "Now Ms. Pearlman, directing your attention to 2:30 pm on

September 23, 2018 in Aurora, Illinois, did you have occasion to speak with Officer McNulty when he responded to your apartment?"

A: "Yes."

Q: "And in that conversation did he ask you what happened?"

A: "Yes he did."

Q: "And did you tell him..."

The true gold is here with the 2nd C. Young attorneys want to quickly rush through the elements to get to confronting the witness faster. They want to start waving the prior inconsistent statement underneath the witness's nose and start waving it around in front of the jury.

But that's not where the gold is at. The gold is in the middle section when the attorney gets the witness to confirm the surrounding circumstances of the statement. The witness is likely to give all that up without a fight because the questions feel harmless. Taken as a whole, however, the detailed circumstances of the statement can be extremely persuasive.

Consider Ms. Pearlman from above who is saying her boyfriend never hit her. The prosecution could have confirmed the details of the statement this way.

Q: "Now Ms. Pearlman, let's go back to the afternoon of September, 23, 2018. Did the police come to your apartment?

A: "Yes."

Q: "That's right, they came to your apartment in Aurora located at 123 Mains Street, correct?"

A: "Yeah."

Q: "It was around 2:30 pm?"

A: "That sounds right."

Q: "You live there with your boyfriend?"

A: "You know I do."

Q: "The police came because they were called is that true?"

A: "Yup."

Q: "In fact, it was you that called the police right?"

A: "I did. I called them 'cause I was upset."

Q: "You called the police after an argument with your boyfriend, correct?"

A: "Yes, but he didn't do nothing."

Q: "When the police got there you were upset?"

A: "I was mad."

Q: "You were crying and emotional?"

A: "I was just upset."

Q: "Officer McNulty was one of the officers who arrived at your apartment?"

A: "I don't know his name, but that sounds like the guy."

Q: "When he got there he asked you some questions, correct?"

A: "He wanted to know what happened."

Q: "And did you tell him at that point that..."

You see when the "commitment" questions are stretched out a bit more it often feels quite benign for the witness to just agree to these innocent details. However, the jury learns more about the details of the conversation and gets a chance to "experience" the conversation a bit more with the victim.

It doesn't matter how the witness answers these foundational questions. The jury is going to be on the ride with you and will have a more complete picture of the circumstances of the statement. In the above example, the jury is going to be wondering why the victim would go to the trouble of calling the police and getting them to her apartment if "nothing happened."

Let's see how the prosecution could lay the 2nd C foundation questions with Marlo. After Marlo commits to his story that Omar didn't fight with anyone that night, the prosecution has to get right into the circumstances of the earlier statement to the police. It could sound like this:

Q: "I mean you spoke to an officer that night, didn't you?"

A: "I mean, I guess. They just asked me a question."

Q: "It was right after the shooting?"

A: "Yeah, right before the bar closed."

Q: "What was it, a little after 2 am?"

A: "That's when they close."

Q: "This was on September 23, 2018?"

A: "Yup."

Q: "When you came out of the bar you were standing in the parking lot?

A: "Everybody was out there."

Q: "You had a chance to see the guy lying on the ground and bleeding?"

A: "Yeah, by the time I got out there the firemen were already helping him."

Q: "You didn't know who it was, did you?"

A: "Wasn't sure."

Q: "But you were able to see it wasn't Omar lying on the ground, right?"

A: "I knew it wasn't Omar."

Q: "Omar was with you earlier in the bar?"

A: "We's together."

Q: "That's when an officer approached you and asked if you saw anything or if you know the victim?"

A: "I'm not sure what he said."

At this point, Marlo is prepped and ready to be confronted with his earlier statement to the police. Can you see how the witness is likely to admit to all these "innocent" foundation questions?

Marlo is likely to answer all these questions without a hitch even though he ultimately denies saying the statement. It doesn't matter. The jury is easily going to see, feel, and understand the nature of the circumstances of the statement.

The jury will see that Marlo was just relieved his buddy was not the one on the ground and will understand his guard was down when he answered the officer's question.

It's here with the 2nd C where true persuasion is really possible. This is where the trial gold is at.

Third C (Confront) - Finally the 3rd C is when you confront the witness with the prior inconsistent statement. It's when you finally get to reveal exactly what the witness said in the prior statement.

There is also a very specific way to do this. You have to lay it out in an exact and deliberate fashion <u>with leading questions</u>. Not only does it need to be specific, but the language in the question should track the exact verbiage of the statement. This often means reading the exact words of the statement right off a prepared document.

It's done this way to make sure that you only get in the elements of the statement that should be coming in. There is no room for creativity here. Confrontation is all about sticking to what's on the paper.

If we finish up the confrontation with Marlo, the prosecutor could do it this way:

Q: "At that time did you answer the officer's question by saying, 'Not really. It's nobody I know?'"

A: "I mean, I guess I might have said that. I actually don't remember."

Q: "Did you also tell the officer at that time that, 'It's just some guy my homie, Omar, whooped-up for rapping on his girl, Betty?'"

A: "Nah, man. No way I told him that."

Pretty simple stuff. If we go back to our domestic violence example. We can pick up with the confrontation of the victim like this:

Q: "And did you tell him, 'I live here with my boyfriend, Ronald?'"

A: "I may have told him that."

Q: "And did you tell him, 'we got in an argument over text messages and he got very upset?'"

A: "Yes, I said that."

Q: "And did you tell him, 'when I went for the door to leave the apartment he grabbed me and turned me around?'"

A: "Yes."

Q: "And did you tell the officer, 'when I turned around he punched and slapped me?'"

A: "I said that, but it wasn't true. I was very upset over everything."

Q: "And did you tell him that, 'I was able to get away and call the police?'"

A: "Yes."

That's it, you're done. You have to be very specific when you finally confront the witness, and let me say again:

You should only use leading questions.

This isn't all that complicated, but it has to be done like this. Keeping the questions tight is a matter of fundamental fairness to the witness and the other side. Very specific and leading questions ensure that nothing improper or inaccurate makes it into the record. You also limit the impeachment to only what was actually said. When it's done this way it makes for a better proceeding.

Opposing counsel can't be there when the original out-of-court statement was made. However, the next best thing is to be allowed to ask the witness any details they want to ask about the prior inconsistent statement.

In this domestic violence example from above opposing counsel is going to have the chance to ask the witness any follow-up questions they may have. It's up to opposing counsel, but they get the chance if they want it. If the attorney wants to she may ask,

"Why did you tell the police your boyfriend punched and slapped you?"

They are free to ask that question. The witness will have a chance to explain the original statement <u>if and only if opposing counsel allows it</u>.

When impeachment with the three C's is done properly and accurately it can be extremely persuasive in front of a jury. It looks good and feels good when you nail it.

The Impeaching Witness

After a witness has been confronted with a prior inconsistent statement, the witness has two choices. The witness can admit that they made the prior statement or deny it. If the witness admits that they said the prior statement, we say the impeachment has been "perfected." The process is now complete.

On the other hand, if the witness denies making the statement, the attorney conducting the impeachment is now obligated to "perfect" the impeachment. This can only be done by calling another witness to the stand who can corroborate the making of the statement. This additional witness is called an "impeachment witness."

The attorney conducting the impeachment obviously has no idea if the witness is going to admit to making the statement or deny it. Therefore, the attorney needs to have the "impeachment witness" lined-up and ready to testify in the event that the witness denies making the statement.

It is improper for an attorney who is not prepared to "perfect" the impeachment with an "impeaching witness" to ask the witness about the prior inconsistent statement. The attorney can't ask the questions if they are not ready to prove up the prior statement.

Remember, prior inconsistent statements are still out-of-court statements. They are still treated like a vial containing the plague and the black death. They are a little dangerous and need to be handled with caution.

An attorney unprepared to prove up the prior statement is not allowed to bring it up willy-nilly, just like that, like it's an afterthought. There is still a danger that a jury could give the statement unjustified weight, so it's incumbent on the attorney to establish that the statement was made. If the attorney can't do this, then they can't complete their impeachment and have no right to even attempt it.

Affirmative Damage Rule

Finally, there is one last little twist with classical impeachment.

Recall that impeachment means to cancel out. It's often the attorney on cross-examination that is trying to discredit a witness. More and more, however, attorneys find themselves calling witnesses on direct-examination who testify inconsistently with a prior statement.

There is an additional concern involving attorneys who attempt to impeach their own witness. A "sneaky" lawyer might call a witness even though they're pretty confident the witness is going to testify inconsistently with a prior statement.

Why would a lawyer call a witness they are pretty sure is going to "flip" on them like this? Why, to impeach them, of course.

A lawyer who knows his witness is going south might call the witness to the stand anyway just so they can impeach the witness with a prior inconsistent statement. When we are dealing with pure impeachment, when the statement has no substantive value, this practice is frowned upon.

This is discouraged because it seems to needlessly expose the jury to an unreliable out-of-court statement. To try to limit this practice, the "affirmative damage" rule was born.

The "affirmative damage" rule has been stated this way:

> *"A court's witness, or any witness for that matter, cannot be impeached by prior inconsistent statements unless his testimony has damaged, rather than failed to support the position of the impeaching party. The reason for this is simple: No possible reason exists to impeach a witness who has not contradicted any of the impeaching party's evidence, except to bring inadmissible hearsay to the attention of the jury. Impeachment is supposed to cancel out the witness' testimony. It is only when the witness' testimony is more damaging than his complete failure to testify would have been that impeachment is useful."*

People v. Weaver, 92 Ill.2d 545, 563 (1982). How is a witness "damaging" to a party's position? In regards to what is considered "damaging," the *Cruz* court said that:

> "'Damage,' as referred to in Weaver, does not occur where a party interrogates a witness about a fact which would be favorable to the examiner if true, but then receives a reply which is merely negative in its effect on the examiner's case. Such testimony is merely disappointing and not damaging since the examiner's case is no worse off than if the witness had not testified."

People v. Cruz, 162 Ill. 2d 314, 359-60 (1994). There is a distinction here between testimony that is damaging and testimony that is merely disappointing. A witness has damaged a party if the witness changes their testimony in such a way that the party would have been better off had they not called the witness.

This is in contrast to a witness who gets on the stand and merely testifies that they "don't remember" the details of whatever they were called to testify about. In this case the party is not affirmatively damaged by the witness. The witness has just disappointed the party calling the witness.

A witness could also get on the stand and say something fundamentally different. For instance, an alibi witness who doesn't remember if he was with the defendant the night of the murder is one thing.

However, if that witness gets on the stand and testifies that he does remember the night, and the defendant was never with him that night. That's pretty damaging to the defense. It goes way beyond just disappointing the defense. Had the defense known their alibi witness was going to say that they likely would have never called the witness. They would have been better off by not doing so.

This is what we mean by damaging a party and merely disappointing them. A witness who gets on the stand and says, "I don't remember" leaves the party in exactly the same situation they would have been in had they never called the witness. In that sense, the party is no worse off. The party is not damaged by the witness but is merely disappointed.

Witnesses are unpredictable creatures. You never know exactly how they'll testify. In regards to this discussion, testimony from a witness on the stand who says,

"I don't remember,"

is, in terms of disappointing to the party who called the witness, equivalent to testimony like,

"I don't recall."

"It's been so long, I'm not completely sure."

"I'm not positive about things."

"If you say so, but I don't know."

All of these are equivalent statements. Point is, equivocation on the stand comes in all different forms. All this testimony is merely disappointing to a party and is not necessarily damaging to their case. In this sense it is all equivalent to testifying that they "forgot."

You may be aware of Illinois Rule of Evidence 804(a)(3) which states that "unavailability as a witness" includes situations in which the declarant testifies to a lack of memory on the subject matter of the declarant's statement."

This is all fine and true. I'm not trying to turn-over the apple cart. In the last chapter you'll find some resources that provide more information on the "unavailability" of witnesses. Suffice it to say, the vast majority of witnesses who testify are likely to remember some things and be less clear about other topics.

The point is "not remembering," in and of itself, is not damaging.

That's what we have to remember.

Here's another example to consider. Let's say we have a grandma who tells the police that on a certain day her grandson came home around midnight, and he had mud and blood on his clothes. There was a murder victim that same night who also had mud and blood on her clothes.

Grandma testifies at trial. She says,

"I don't remember nothing about my grandson from that night."

In this case, the state is disappointed. They are no better off had they just not called Grandma. Their case has not been damaged. If instead she testifies that,

"I did see him that night, he was home in bed the entire night, he'd been sick."

Not only is the state disappointed in Grandma, their case has also now been affirmatively damaged. Grandma is changing her testimony in a fundamental way. Now she is starting to provide an alibi.

The prosecution is worse off for calling grandma to the witness stand. They would have been better off keeping her away from the stand. The state can now impeach Grandma. In the first example, the state <u>would not be allowed</u> to impeach her with her prior inconsistent statement.

Under classical impeachment, a party calling a witness is only allowed to impeach that witness when the witness has affirmatively damaged the party.

A party is not allowed to impeach a witness with a prior inconsistent statement if that witness has merely disappointed the party.

It's important to remember that the "affirmative damage" rule only applies to the party that called the witness. The opposing party is free to impeach a witness regardless of the distinction between disappointing and damaging their case.

Good-Faith Basis

It might be helpful to revisit the discussion concerning the "impeaching witness."

There is a difference between the existence of extrinsic evidence that can be used to impeach a witness and having a good-faith basis to ask a question. In the context of a prior inconsistent statement, the extrinsic evidence is obviously the statement itself. It also includes the witness who can establish that the prior statement was uttered by the initial witness.

In the realm of impeaching a witness with a prior inconsistent statement, the rules require that the attorney have a good-faith basis that the prior statement was said. Having a good-faith means much more than simply being aware of the existence of the statement.

A good-faith basis means the impeaching attorney, if needed, can prove up the prior inconsistent statement with an impeaching witness. It means that you are not only aware of the prior statement, but you are also ready and able to prove the statement with extrinsic evidence.

In other words, you are ready to prove up the prior inconsistent statement independently of the witness being impeached. If the witness under examination denies making the statement, you have to establish that it was said by some other means.

Quite often, an experienced and aware trial judge might interrupt your questioning to ask,

"Excuse me counsel, where is Officer McNulty?"

That question might seem to come out of left field. The judge is essentially asking you if you have a good-faith basis to proceed down the line of impeachment the judge feels is coming. The judge is really asking,

> "Do you have a good-faith basis that you can perfect the impeachment if you need to? If this witness denies making the statement will you be able to perfect that impeachment by proving-up the statement right here, right now?"

The good-faith basis requirement is shorthand for this requirement. Attorneys versed in this concept can quite easily shut down an avenue of questioning if they know the other side has not gone to the trouble of lining up the impeachment witness.

What the judge wants to hear is that the officer is in the hallway ready to come in, if you need him, to perfect the impeachment you're about to get into with the witness.

If instead you tell the judge that Officer McNulty is on a tour in Afghanistan, the judge is going to shut you down and not allow you to get into the impeachment. You can't ask a single question about a prior inconsistent statement if you are not able and ready to perfect it.

You never know what a witness is going to say on the stand. You can't be sure the witness is going to admit to making the prior statement. You can't plan for that. What you have to plan for is the possibility that the witness says,

"No, I never said that."

At that moment, under the rules you are now obligated to perfect your impeachment with extrinsic evidence of the prior inconsistent statement.

Be ready to deal with all kinds of havoc from the judge and opposing counsel if you begin to impeach a witness with a prior inconsistent statement you are not prepared to prove up with an impeaching witness. You'll quickly find yourself in a heap of trouble. This is exactly a situation where you'll have to deal with a motion for a mistrial.

The point is you have to be prepared.

To say you've got knowledge of extrinsic evidence of a prior inconsistent statement because you read it in a report somewhere is not good enough. Judges aren't impressed by that. Your good-faith basis means you have a witness who can testify to complete the impeachment and that witness is present and ready to get on the stand if needed.

Asking impeachment questions without the ability to perfect it is considered highly improper.

The reason this is considered improper is because we accept the jury is going to be influenced by the mere asking of the questions about the prior inconsistent statement. The jury will believe you wouldn't have asked the question if you didn't have some reason to ask it.

In other words, merely by asking the question you win some points, and this may be improper if you are not ready to follow through all the way. You are not entitled to those free points if you are not ready to establish the making of the statement.

It's improper to win points you can't independently establish. That's why this is improper. Not only is it improper, it is sufficient in itself to be plain error and result in a reversal.

Final Thoughts

As you can imagine, this version of the impeachment rule had its problems.

The rule rested on a legal fantasy that juries could tell the difference between "impeachment only" testimony and "substantive evidence" testimony. The discussion above illustrates that the rule-makers understood that a jury was likely to treat any testimony they heard in court as substantive evidence.

It's very difficult to put the cat back in the bag once it's been let out.

Telling an attorney to only argue a statement for impeachment value and not the substantive evidentiary value is one thing but expecting a jury to be able to tell the difference is quite another thing.

The law needed a little tweaking. If attorneys were hell bent into finding ways for a jury to hear about a prior inconsistent statement then the rules needed to be adapted to allow for some prior inconsistent statements that could be used as substantive evidence.

This is when 725 ILCS 5/115-10.1 entered the picture.

6

The Statute & The Rules of Evidence

We saw how classical impeachment evolved without the rules. Today we have the benefit of the written word.

The written rules don't completely throw away the old ideas. They are built into the current system. The traditional elements are still there.

However, the new rules try to expand the truth seeking function of the trial process. They still treat prior out-of-court statements as something that should be treated with great caution. But if you wear gloves and follow the rules, no one will get hurt.

Here are the current Illinois rules and statutes on impeachment followed by a few remarks on how they should be interpreted.

Illinois Rule of Evidence Rule 613.
PRIOR STATEMENTS OF WITNESSES

(a) **Examining Witness Concerning Prior Statement.** In

examining a witness concerning a prior statement made by the witness, whether written or not, the statement need not be shown nor its contents disclosed to the witness at that time, but on request the same shall be shown or disclosed to opposing counsel.

(b) Extrinsic Evidence of Prior Inconsistent Statement of Witness. Extrinsic evidence of a prior inconsistent statement by a witness is not admissible unless the witness is first afforded an opportunity to explain or deny the same and the opposing party is afforded an opportunity to interrogate the witness thereon, or the interests of justice otherwise require. This provision does not apply to admissions statements of a party-opponent as defined in Rule 801(d)(2).

(c) ...

(Adopted September 27, 2010, eff. January 1, 2011; amended Jan. 6, 2015, eff. immediately; amended Oct. 15, 2015, eff. immediately.)

Federal Rule of Evidence 613 is identical to the Illinois rule.

Rule 613(b) is generally considered to have captured the classical form of impeachment. It covers pure impeachment, which has no substantive evidence component. It includes the old 3 C's foundational requirement for impeaching a witness with a prior inconsistent statement.

The prior inconsistent statement is the "extrinsic evidence" referenced in the section. The prior statement is the outside evidence that can be brought in to establish that the witness under examination said something different in the past.

Section (b) does not explicitly mention the 3 C's or the RAC system, but it's all there. That's what it is all about. Affording the witness "an opportunity to explain or deny the same" is essentially the first C. The second C (confirming the time, place, and circumstance of the statement) is not explicitly mentioned. Nonetheless, you know you have to do it because you have to alert the witness to the time, place, and circumstance of the statement.

The rule also makes it clear that opposing counsel has a chance to cross examine the witness about the prior statement. No surprise there. If the problem with these statements is that counsel cannot be there when they are made, well then, the rules will at least allow counsel to ask as many questions as they want about the making of the statement.

There is nothing special happening in 613(a). It looks like they just want to make it clear that you don't have to let the witness under examination actually see on paper the prior inconsistent statement that is about to be shoved down their throat.

That was never a practice among trial attorneys. 613(a) makes it clear you don't have to hand over your notes to the witness. If opposing counsel wants to see paper on the statement, sure, you hand it over. No biggie.

Let's move on to where the real magic is happening in Illinois. For this we turn not to a rule of evidence, but we go to the Illinois Code of Criminal Procedure.

THE STATUTE & THE RULES OF EVIDENCE

725 ILCS 5/115-10.1.
Admissibility of Prior Inconsistent Statements

In all criminal cases, evidence of a statement made by a witness is not made inadmissible by the hearsay rule if

(a) the statement is inconsistent with his testimony at the hearing or trial, and

(b) the witness is subject to cross-examination concerning the statement, and

(c) the statement—

(1) was made under oath at a trial, hearing, or other proceeding, or

(2) narrates, describes, or explains an event or condition of which the witness had personal knowledge, and

(A) the statement is proved to have been written or signed by the witness, or

(B) the witness acknowledged under oath the making of the statement either in his testimony at the hearing or trial in which the admission into evidence of the prior statement is being sought, or at a trial, hearing, or other proceeding, or

(C) the statement is proved to have been accurately recorded by a tape recorder, videotape recording, or any other similar electronic means of sound recording.

Nothing in this Section shall render a prior inconsistent statement inadmissible for purposes of impeachment because such statement was not recorded or otherwise fails to meet the criteria set forth herein.

(Source: P.A. 83-1042.)

With this statute the legislature set up certain conditions that, when met, turn impeachment with prior inconsistent statement into substantive evidence.

How did they do that?

They did it by simply defining a prior inconsistent statement that meets the requirements set out in the code as **not being hearsay.** If it's not hearsay it means it can be treated like any other good, old-fashioned piece of evidence. It means the substance of the prior inconsistent statement magically transforms into substantive evidence.

The rule took special care to make sure not just *any* prior inconsistent statement would be treated like this. It's just certain special ones.

The special ones are the statements we know for sure were actually uttered by the witness. This way we minimize the risk of letting into evidence an unreliable statement that may never have been stated in the first place.

If the prior statement was...

- sworn to in a prior hearing or trial,
- if it was recorded, written down, or signed by the witness, or
- if the witness acknowledges under oath that they made the statement,

then we know for sure that the statement was actually made.

This statute is a game changer for impeachment. The statute was created by prosecutors who pushed it into existence. They were the ones who frequently found themselves in trials with witnesses who had "flipped" on them. You'll notice the statute only applies in criminal cases.

However, later we'll discuss in detail how the statute doesn't specifically say that *only* prosecutors can use it. The law is broader than that. Any criminal defense attorney is free to use and apply the statute if they see fit.

Just to make sure the concept of substantive evidence by prior inconsistent statements never goes away, the Illinois Supreme Court created a rule of evidence that says the same thing as 725 ILCS 5/115-101. Here's the evidentiary rule that copied the statute. They put it in the Illinois hearsay definition section. It looks like this:

Illinois Rule of Evidence Rule 801.
DEFINITIONS

The following definitions apply under this article:

(a) **Statement**. A "statement" is (1) an oral or written assertion or (2) nonverbal conduct of a person, if it is intended by the person as an assertion.

(b) **Declarant**. A "declarant" is a person who makes a statement.

(c) **Hearsay**. "Hearsay" is a statement, other than one made by the declarant while testifying at the trial or hearing, offered in evidence to prove the truth of the matter asserted.

(d) **Statements Which Are Not Hearsay**. A statement is not hearsay if

(1) **Prior Statement by Witness.** In a criminal case, the declarant testifies at the trial or hearing and is subject to cross-examination concerning the statement, and the statement is

(A) inconsistent with the declarant's testimony at the trial or hearing, and—

(1) was made under oath at a trial, hearing, or other proceeding, or in a deposition, or

(2) narrates, describes, or explains an event or condition of which the declarant had personal knowledge, and

(a) the statement is proved to have been written or signed by the declarant, or

(b) the declarant acknowledged under oath the making of the statement either in the declarant's testimony at the hearing or trial in which the admission into evidence of the prior statement is being sought or at a trial, hearing, or other proceeding, or in a deposition, or

(c) the statement is proved to have been accurately recorded by a tape recorder, videotape recording, or any other similar electronic means of sound recording; or

(B) one of identification of a person made after perceiving the person.

(2) ....

(Adopted September 27, 2010, eff. January 1, 2011; amended Oct. 15, 2015, eff. immediately.)

Illinois Rule of Evidence 801(d)(1) does the exact same thing as 725 ILCS 5/115-10.1. It's redundant, but I guess it means this rule isn't changing anytime soon.

In the federal system they have the same rule. The Federal Rule of Evidence 801(d) looks like this:

Federal Rule of Evidence 801. Definitions That Apply to This Article; Exclusions from Hearsay

(d) **Statements That Are Not Hearsay**. A statement that meets the following conditions is not hearsay:

(1) *A Declarant-Witness' Prior Statement.* The declarant testifies and is subject to cross-examination about a prior statement, and the statement:

(A) is inconsistent with the declarant's testimony and was given under penalty of perjury at a trial, hearing, or other proceeding or in a deposition...

(Pub. L. 93–595, §1, Jan. 2, 1975, 88 Stat. 1938; Pub. L. 94–113, §1, Oct. 16, 1975, 89 Stat. 576; Mar. 2, 1987, eff. Oct. 1, 1987; Apr. 11, 1997, eff. Dec. 1, 1997; Apr. 26, 2011, eff. Dec. 1, 2011; Apr. 25, 2014, eff. Dec. 1, 2014.)

The federal rule leads to the same result. The biggest difference is that in the federal system the rule also applies in civil cases.

It's worth taking a moment to reflect on the significance of 725 ILCS 5/115-10.1 and Illinois Rule of Evidence 801(d)(1). Since the dawn of man we have been perfecting and improving our technology.

So too, we have been tweaking and adapting our laws and our rules of evidence. The idea of substantive evidence from a prior inconsistent statement should not be taken for granted. Its significance should be noted.

For so long in our history this was not the case. This means a trier of fact is permitted to go beyond solely disbelieving a witness' testimony and is now permitted to give substantive weight to the witness' prior inconsistent statement.

If the elements of the statute are met, lawyers may encourage the trier of fact to base its decision upon the substance of the prior inconsistent statement.

That's huge.

Illinois has one important difference from the federal rule. When it comes to substantive prior inconsistent statements, the Illinois version of the rule contains the language, "acknowledged under oath the making of the statement."

This means that a statement that is not recorded or written down or made in a prior trial or hearing can still be treated substantively if the witness acknowledges in open court that they made the statement. This option doesn't exist in the same way in the federal system.

We'll talk more about it later.

The important thing to know is that classical impeachment is not dead. It has not been completely replaced by the statute. There is an entire class of out-of-court statements that doesn't meet the requirements of the statute.

The best way to think about this is that impeachment with a prior inconsistent statement that meets the statute is like a souped-up version of classical impeachment. It's better.

But if the statute can't be met, you fall back to relying on classical impeachment the way we've always understood it.

Interestingly, the procedure for executing impeachment with a prior inconsistent statement under 725 ILCS 5/115-10.1 takes on exactly the same 3 C's structure as classical impeachment. That hasn't changed at all.

Placing this rule in 801(d)(1) contemplates that this is how it should work. The Illinois Rules of Evidence are saying that if you follow the impeachment procedure as laid out in Rule 613, that impeachment evidence can be argued substantively if Rule 801(d)(1) has been met.

You have to start with Rule 613 before you make it to Rule 801(d)(1). If you are going to impeach a witness, you have to do it using the proper foundation discussed earlier.

I think this has been one of the sources of confusion in this area. Not being clear on the exact relationship between impeachment and a substantive prior inconsistent statement probably has led to many of the mistakes we see in the record.

From this moment forward, to help keep things logical and clear in our mind whenever we use the term "prior inconsistent statement," we mean substantive impeachment by prior inconsistent statement as outlined in 725 ILCS 5/115-10.1. It is much simpler to just use the term "prior inconsistent statement."

The written rules account for both classical impeachment and impeachment with a prior inconsistent statement. We already mentioned the connection between Rule 613 and Rule 801(d)(1).

Similarly, Illinois Rule of Evidence Rule 607 also establishes that classical impeachment remains viable after the creation of the statute. In fact, Rule 607 pertains only to classical impeachment. Thus, the rule recognizes that classical impeachment remains viable after the statute. Here's what rule 607 says:

Illinois Rule of Evidence Rule 607. WHO MAY IMPEACH

The credibility of a witness may be attacked by any party, including the party calling the witness, except that the credibility of a witness may be attacked by the party calling the witness by means of a prior inconsistent statement only upon a showing of affirmative damage. The foregoing exception does not apply to statements admitted pursuant to Rules 801(d)(1)(A), 801(d)(1)(B), 801(d)(2), or 803.

(Adopted September 27, 2010, eff. January 1, 2011.)

The title of Rule 607 makes it clear we are talking only about impeachment. Additionally, to a certain extent, Rule 607 also applies in a civil courtroom. We know this because the Illinois Supreme Court created separate rules for civil cases. In the "Rules on Civil Proceedings in the Trial Court" you'll find this rule:

Illinois Rule of Evidence Rule 238.
Impeachment of Witnesses; Hostile Witnesses

(a) The credibility of a witness may be attacked by any party, including the party calling the witness.

(b) If the court determines that a witness is hostile or unwilling, the witness may be examined by the party calling the witness as if under cross-examination.

(Amended February 19, 1982, effective April 1, 1982; amended April 11, 2001, effective immediately.)

Classical impeachment, the kind without any substantive value, is alive and well. These rules make that quite clear. Rule 238 is not identical to Rule 607, but the core of classical impeachment is in both. These two rules make it clear that any side can impeach a witness, even if it's your own witness.

The main difference between Illinois Rule of Evidence 607 and 238 is that in criminal cases the old "affirmative damage" rule survived. The rule still prevents the ploy of calling a witness for the purpose of presenting to the jury a favorable prior inconsistent statement that is not admissible substantively.

If a prior inconsistent statement doesn't meet the elements of 725 ILCS 5/115-10.1 then the party has to account for Rule 607. The affirmative damage requirement is back on the table and must be considered. At the risk of being redundant, let me just say again:

The affirmative damage requirement is not necessary when the prior inconsistent statement is admissible as substantive evidence.

Affirmative damage is a concept that only exists for classical impeachment and has no place in a discussion of prior inconsistent statements.

In other words, if a witness can be impeached with a statement that complies with 613(b) **and** 725 ILCS 5/115-10.1 (and 801(d)(1)) the side calling the witness **can** rely on that statement as substantive evidence even if the witness has merely disappointed the party. The party can still impeach the witness with the prior inconsistent statement.

If 725 ILCS 5/115-10.1 (801(d)(1)) doesn't apply, then the affirmative damage rule is back on the table.

If you're interested, the federal rule looks like this:

Federal Rule of Evidence 607.
Who May Impeach a Witness

Any party, including the party that called the witness, may attack the witness' credibility.

(Pub. L. 93–595, §1, Jan. 2, 1975, 88 Stat. 1934; Mar. 2, 1987, eff. Oct. 1, 1987; Apr. 26, 2011, eff. Dec. 1, 2011.)

When it comes to classical impeachment, the feds dispense

with the old-time rule that you couldn't impeach your own witness. They also got rid of any affirmative damage limitation that continues to be a "thing" in the Illinois version of classical impeachment.

Final Thoughts

We've had a chance to discuss where classical impeachment came from and how it works.

725 ILCS 5/115-10.1 sits on top of all this. Hopefully this history of impeachment is going to help you distinguish it from prior inconsistent statements. Let's now jump into the elements of prior inconsistent statements.

7

The Elements Of A Prior Inconsistent Statement

Just Like Classical Impeachment

At this point, we know that prior inconsistent statements work remarkably similar to classical impeachment. The 3 C's are still alive and well. Classical impeachment is still a thing in the modern era, and to properly execute impeachment by prior inconsistent you rely on the same procedure.

You do the same thing for both.

Obviously, the main difference between the two is that with a prior inconsistent statement you get the benefit of substantive evidence. With classical impeachment you do not. Either way, you follow the same procedure.

Additionally, with a prior inconsistent statement you have to

THE ELEMENTS OF A PRIOR INCONSISTENT STATEMENT

make sure you include the elements from the statute. This means that during the Second C, when you are confirming the time, place, and circumstance of the statement, you must ask about the additional elements from the statute. With one or more questions you must demonstrate...

- That the prior statement "was made under oath at a trial, hearing, or other proceeding" or
- Show that it was "written or signed by the witness" or
- The "statement is proved to have been accurately recorded by a tape recorder, videotape recording, or any other similar electronic means of sound recording" or
- That the "the witness acknowledged under oath the making of the statement."

The questioning must also make it clear that the witness had **personal knowledge** of the items being discussed in the statement.

It is the responsibility of the attorney who is conducting the impeachment to make sure that they cover in their questioning the required elements that establish the prior inconsistent statement as substantive evidence.

Opposing counsel isn't going to do you any favors. You also can't rely on the judge to help you if you forget to ask important foundational questions.

You cannot take for granted that everyone will "just know" that you're referring to a written or recorded statement. That is your job to make sure you include these foundational questions when you begin to impeach a witness.

Threshold Issues

If you look at the statute (725 ILCS 5/115-10.1), it begins by establishing that the prior out-of-court statement must be inconsistent with the current testimony. This is a threshold issue you must consider.

This is the starting point.

In my experience, this requirement really doesn't cause problems for most attorneys. Attorneys have no trouble identifying inconsistent statements. This is something that is almost always recognized instantly.

More often than not this isn't going to hang you up in a trial. Nonetheless, you have to be ready for the situations where somebody tries to "impeach" a witness with a supposedly "inconsistent" statement. You have to be ready to shut it down when the other party can't establish the inconsistency.

The statute also makes it clear a witness must be "subject to cross-examination concerning the statement." This requirement will also rarely be an issue for you at trial.

If the witness is in court and on the stand answering questions, then you know they are available for cross. You know you might have issues if you have a witness who is so emotionally debilitated that he or she can't form words. In my experience, this is rare; but it can happen.

You may also have a witness who is claiming some kind of privilege. Again, this can happen. But it's rare.

You have to be ready to deal with these issues if you see it in your trial. Make sure to look at the links at the end of this book to find additional resources on this topic. I won't spend more time on it here because that is an "advanced" topic. The goal now is to cover the basics.

For the most part, if your witness is in court and on the stand they are available. The rule makes it clear that opposing counsel gets a chance for cross-examination on the prior statement.

Bar Shooting In The Early Morning Example

Impeachment with prior inconsistent statement is one of those topics that is best learned by example.

In criminal cases it's quite common to have a witness "flip" his story by the time trial comes along. This happens for many reasons, but let's consider a different example of a shooting in the early morning hours outside a bar. The facts are little different from the last bar shooting example we talked about.

This time imagine the police recorded a statement from a witness. What hasn't changed is the level of cooperation the witness is providing. A lot of times witnesses to crime are not friends of law enforcement.

The witness in this example is the only eyewitness to the shooting. The crime happened in the early morning hours outside a bar. When the state calls the witness at trial, he has changed his tune and testifies that,

"I don't remember."

Now, the prosecutor is sitting there knowing there's a recorded statement of this witness where he is on tape telling the police that he saw a guy with a Pittsburgh Steelers jersey walk out of the bar at 2:30 a.m. and start shooting his gun at cars passing by.

In this example, the prosecutor's instinct is going to be to ask this question,

"Didn't you make a recorded statement where you told police you saw a man in a Steelers jersey shoot at cars passing by?"

...and that would be wrong.

That won't fly.

If the prosecutor tried to do it that way, opposing counsel or even the judge would shut it down for not following the proper foundation. The moment the witness says he doesn't remember, the prosecutor has to kick into the proper foundational questions.

The prosecutor has to break it down and follow the 3 C's. Instead the prosecutor should begin the impeachment process by asking

THE ELEMENTS OF A PRIOR INCONSISTENT STATEMENT

these questions,

Q: "Did you say you remember everything?"

A: "No. I said I don't remember what happened that night."

Q: "To be clear, we're talking about 2:30 am on September 23, 2018, correct?"

A: "Yeah, that's what you said."

Q: "And you were outside the Blue's Tavern located in Aurora, Illinois on that night?"

A: "You know I already said I was there."

Q: "That was the night the police picked you up and took you to the police station?"

A: "They picked me up for doing nothing."

Q: "They arrested you didn't they?"

A: "Sure did, for nothing."

Q: "They searched you and locked you in an interrogation room, didn't they?"

A: "Yeah, they did."

Q: "But you didn't have anything illegal on you, right?"

A: "Nah man, I wasn't holding nothing but my wallet, and that ain't illegal."

Q: "They had you for what, 20 minutes?"

A: "Felt longer."

Q: "But they did let you go right?"

A: "Eventually, when they figured out I didn't do nothing."

Q: "You helped them figure that out, didn't you?"

A: "I mean I guess, I was telling them I didn't do anything."

Q: "In the interrogation room, where they took you, you spoke to a detective about why they picked you up?"

A: "I mean yes, I guess. I remember talking to the police. I just don't remember everything that happened that night."

Q: "The police asked you questions about what you saw outside the tavern?"

A: "Yes. They was asking."

Q: "And for 20 minutes, maybe longer, you talked to the detectives about what happened outside the Blue's Tavern on September 23, 2018 around 2:30 am?"

THE ELEMENTS OF A PRIOR INCONSISTENT STATEMENT

A: "Yeah, but I don't remember."

Q: "This conversation with the detectives, it was recorded right?"

A: "They put a recorder or something on the table, and they said they were going to record everything, but I don't know about electronics and stuff."

At this point, the prosecutor has gotten through the second C. All that is left is to confront the witness. The confrontation also has to be tight and in the form of a leading question.

More likely than not, it will be a series of leading questions making sure the exact words used by the witness are parroted in the question. This is not the time for open-ended questions. Confrontation might sound like this,

Q: "In that conversation right before the police let you go, didn't you tell them you 'was outside Blues's just chillin' drinking a 40?'"

A: "I don't remember that."

Q: "Didn't you tell the detective you saw 'a tall white dude come out Blue's?'"

A: "I don't remember."

Q: "Didn't you tell the detective the tall white dude 'was wearing a knee-long Pittsburgh Steelers jersey?'"

A: "I don't remember."

Q: "Didn't you tell the detective that the tall white dude cracked me up 'cause it was like he was lifting his dress when he pulled a glock from his belt?'"

A: "That do sound funny, but I don't remember."

Q: "Didn't you then tell the detective that the tall white dude 'just started popping at cars going by for no reason'?"

A: "I don't remember."

At this point, you are done with the witness.

It doesn't matter that the witness denies making the statement. The prosecution just needs to perfect the impeachment by calling the detective that recorded the interview. Had the witness admitted to the statements then the impeachment would be complete.

Perfecting the impeachment with the officer would sound like this,

Q: "Detective, what's your name? Who do you work for?"

A: "I'm Detective McNulty. I'm a detective with the Aurora Police Department's Violent Crimes Unit."

Q: "Did you investigate a shooting that occurred outside Blue's

THE ELEMENTS OF A PRIOR INCONSISTENT STATEMENT

Tavern in downtown Aurora on September the 23rd around 2:30 am?"

A: "Yes, I did."

Q: "Did you have the chance to question Omar Little shortly thereafter in an Aurora PD interrogation room?"

A: "Yes, I talked to him."

Q: "Was this conversation recorded?"

At this point, the prosecutor could either produce the recording, lay a foundation for it and play it for the jury, or the prosecutor can just have the officer get into the statement.

These questions to the officer also have to be direct, leading, and tight. Only the substance of the statement and nothing else should be covered. Again, this is not the time for open-ended questions. The impeachment perfection would sound like this,

Q: "In this interview, did Omar Little tell you that 'I was outside Blue's just chillin' drinking a 40?'"

A: "Yes."

Q: "In this interview did Omar Little tell you that 'I seen this tall white dude come out Blue's?'"

A: "Yes, he said that."

Q: "In this interview did Omar Little tell you that the man 'was wearing a knee-long Pittsburgh Steelers jersey?'"

A: "Yes."

Q: "In this interview did Omar Little tell you that this tall white man in the Steelers Jersey 'cracked me up 'cause it was like he was lifting his dress when he pulled a glock from his belt?'"

A: "He said that, and he chuckled as he said it."

Q: "In this interview did Omar Little tell you that 'the tall white dude just started popping at cars going by for no reason?'"

A: "Yes, that's what he said."

At this point, you have just perfected the impeachment. If you want to play the recording for the jury rather than ask the questions from above you'd instead hand the witness the exhibit and say,

Q: "Detective McNulty do you recognize People's Exhibit 23?"

A: "Yes, it's the CD of the recording with Omar Little on September 23."

Q: "You've had a chance to listen to the recording?"

A: "Yes, I have."

Q: "Does it fairly and accurately reflect the interview with Omar

THE ELEMENTS OF A PRIOR INCONSISTENT STATEMENT

Little?"

A: "Yes, it does."

Q: "Your Honor, at this time I'd move to admit People's Exhibit 23 into evidence."

J: "It's admitted."

Then you'd publish the recording, making sure to play only the statement outlined above. This likely means the CD had to be redacted and edited before trial.

This sounded and looked like classical impeachment. However, because the foundation for the impeachment included the additional element that the interview was recorded that means the substance of the interview can be considered as substantive evidence in the case against the defendant.

Since this was the only eyewitness to the shooting, the prosecutor would have been in quite the pickle if they didn't know how to execute the impeachment.

It's understandable that the prosecution's first instinct is to confront the witness with the prior statement right from the get-go. But they can't do that.

"Didn't you make a recorded statement where you told police you saw a man in a Steelers jersey shoot at cars passing by?"

Had they done that without going back and laying down the

proper foundation questions, either the judge or opposing counsel could have quickly shut down this line of questioning. If that happened, there would have been no real evidence for the state to rest its case on.

In this example, it was crucial that the state properly admit the prior inconsistent statement because the entire case rested on that prior statement. Therefore it is crucial they do it the right way.

Juries don't seem to have a problem with this.

But you have to lay the proper foundation. It's not enough nor sufficient that the police recorded the statement. If the statute and the rules are not complied with, it won't matter. You must comply with the technicalities of the statute and the rules.

Once you understand this you'll see it's really not that tricky.

It's just very specific. One just has to figure out how to do it and do it properly. Learn it. Stick to the program and get it rote in your mind. You have to be ready for the opportunity to flow into the 3 C's when the opportunity presents itself at trial.

Trust me. It inevitably will come up.

The Personal Knowledge Requirement

Now let's briefly address the "personal knowledge" requirement mentioned in 725 ILCS 5/115-10.1.

It is talking about the witness having personal knowledge of what is being described in the statement. This is different from having personal knowledge of the making of the statement.

They are talking about the crime, the thing the trial is about. It is not talking about the fact that the witness remembers the conversation or has personal knowledge of the discussion where the prior inconsistent statement was made. That is not what they mean when they are talking about personal knowledge.

Although it's true that the making of the statement qualifies as an event, the statute is not using the term in this manner. Instead the "personal knowledge" requirement necessitates that the declarant observe the events described in the statement. The events of the crime described in the statement is the "event or condition" described in the statute.

If the rule was otherwise, that would mean an entire section of the statue, section (c)(2) would be superfluous. See *People v. Simpson*, 2015 IL 116512 (January). This interpretation of the "personal knowledge" requirement is pretty solid in the case law. I don't think you need to harp on it too much, but if you want more reading on this topic start with *Simpson*.

What Defense Attorneys Should Know

An important aspect of the statue that bears repeating more than once and that's something most lawyers don't realize is that defense attorneys can also make use of section 725 ILCS 5/115-10.1.

There certainly are times when defense counsel might impeach a witness to demonstrate that a witness is lying. There is nothing unusual about a defense attorney using a prior inconsistent statement to impeach a witness.

The benefit of 725 ILCS 5/115-10.1 is equally valuable for defense attorneys.

Consider a defense attorney's situation when they are only allowed to use a prior statement for impeachment purposes. At closing argument, counsel might argue something along the lines of...

"This witness said that my client did it, but you heard on cross-examination that he wasn't sure and maybe someone else did it."

That's important testimony, but if it can only be used for impeachment, then that's not substantive evidence. Counsel can only argue to the jury that the witness cannot be believed.

Counsel can't argue someone else did it.

The distinction sounds like a fine one to make, but centuries of criminal trials suggest the distinction is fundamentally crucial. As we already know, impeachment-only evidence is offered for the limited purpose of demonstrating that the witness is not telling the truth. It is not substantive evidence of the underlying issue.

Defense attorneys usually are trying to point out where there

THE ELEMENTS OF A PRIOR INCONSISTENT STATEMENT

is reasonable doubt. As the defense, you take what you can get. So when an opportunity to impeach with a prior inconsistent statement presents itself, counsel has to be ready to pounce on that.

There will be instances where counsel for the defense can use a prior inconsistent statement not only to impeach a witness but also use it as substantive evidence. When this happens it has to be treated like a gift and taken advantage of to the maximum.

Being able to tell a jury that an eyewitness says another guy did this crime is powerful evidence. It may be worth the trouble for a defense attorney to conduct an acknowledgment hearing to lock in a witness who is cooperating with the defense for the moment but whose continued cooperation cannot be ensured.

There's no reason defense investigators can't record interviews the exact same way police do it. Counsel has to know what the statute says, know how to use it, and be ready to execute when it's time.

People think 725 ILCS 5/115-10.1 is for the state only, but it says no such thing. Sure, overall it's prosecutors who make the most frequent use of this section of the code. In certain types of crimes, this is the bread and butter for a successful prosecution.

Nonetheless, the statute is also there for the defense. A few defense attorneys are beginning to make use of this section and their clients are better off for it. Understanding the law is the first part, and keeping your eyes open for its application in your case follows after that.

If you are impeaching a witness as a defense attorney with a prior inconsistent statement you should want to bring it out substantively if you can. Use the statute, it's there.

So you call a witness who's going to establish an alibi for your client. Say that your witness gets nervous or he says he doesn't recall, and he simply testifies that,

"I don't remember."

At this point, the defense is free to use the statute just like the state can. That's what the statute is telling you. You get right into your foundation questions, so you have the right to confront the witness with their prior statement.

Q: "Mr. Witness, directing your attention to a specific time, date, and place, did you talk to my investigator, Mr. McNulty, about this case?"

A: "Yes."

Q: "And did he ask you where you were at this specific date and time and whether the defendant was with you?"

A: "Yes, he did."

Q: "And did you tell him that the defendant was with you?"

A: "No, I don't remember that."

THE ELEMENTS OF A PRIOR INCONSISTENT STATEMENT

No problem.

Now you call your investigator to establish that he did say the defendant was with him the night of the shooting. Use the statute just the same way the state would use it.

The problem with most defense attorneys is that they don't have the extrinsic evidence available. They don't have regular investigators like the prosecution.

The extrinsic evidence the defense knows about usually comes from the police reports and usually those aren't the statements that are recorded or written down.

You don't have written, recorded or acknowledged statements because the state didn't give them to you. So go get them yourself.

There is no rule out there that says you can't have it. Go get them. The prosecution doesn't have it because it's not important to their case. They haven't sent their investigators out with a recorder or pen and paper. They are choosing to not apply the rule for a certain witness. Fine. You do it.

The defense doesn't need to rely, nor should it, on the prosecution to gather its evidence. It's incumbent on the defense to get out there and record the important witnesses or run some acknowledgment hearings. It's work. But the other side is not going to do it for you.

Which is why I want to emphasize that defense attorneys can

use 725 ILCS 5/115-10.1 as well.

Here's the takeaway:

> *If you are a defense attorney and you got a big case with a key witness who is very important to you, get paper on the witness. Pin him down on paper just like the police would do with a recording or a written statement. You have them write it. You write it out if they won't and have them sign it. If this witness ends up "flipping" on you while on the stand, you can bring out what he had said in the past. This is a beautiful thing. It was not always available. The statute is here now, so let's start making use of it.*

725 ILCS 5/115-10.1 was written to make a trial more of a truth-seeking process. It seeks to bring out everything a witness has to say about what happened. If a witness has changed his or her story, let the trier of fact decide which of these versions is true.

But it's your job to get the different version in front of the jury. To help you do this, in the next chapter we'll talk about another option available for defense attorneys and prosecutors alike.

8

The Acknowledgment Hearing

Unique To Illinois

The Illinois statute on prior inconsistent statements is a little different than the federal statute. Aside from only being applicable in criminal cases, the Illinois law has this language in subsection (B). It says an out-of-court statement is not hearsay if the witness has

> "...acknowledged under oath the making of the statement either in his testimony at the hearing or trial in which the admission into evidence of the prior statement is being sought, or at a trial, hearing, or other proceeding, or..."

725 ILCS 5/115-10.1(c)(2)(B). This creates a unique and underused opportunity in Illinois criminal cases. The "acknowledgment hearing" is very much an "Illinois thing." This is also called a "*Brothers* hearing" because the topic is discussed in

People v. Brothers, 2015 IL App (4th) 130644 (September).

The gist of the hearing is that a party has a chance to convert a non-substantive prior inconsistent statement into a substantive prior inconsistent statement if the witness acknowledges making the statement. The section provides a mechanism for how to do this.

Brothers is a very interesting case.

It was written by Justice Steigmann. Judge Steigmann actually authored the statute. He's done a lot of work on it. He spearheaded the law's passage. He's written a couple of books on evidence about it. The quote at the beginning of this book is by Judge Steigmann. As you've read, he is one of the appellate court judges who has noted that attorneys keep making mistakes with this issue. In this chapter we'll discuss important information from *Brothers* pertaining to the "acknowledgment hearing."

***Brothers* shows us that in the "acknowledgment hearing" you are essentially creating substantive evidence.**

A Domestic Violence Example

Let's say, for example, we have another domestic violence case where we have a recantation from a victim.

In this example, the victim makes a statement to the police which is mentioned in the police report. No other written or recorded statement of the victim was made. The defense

THE ACKNOWLEDGMENT HEARING

attorney has a good idea that the witness is going to recant. This is a good time to file that type of motion if you are a defendant because you can really cut the state's case out from underneath them.

In any case, it's really important to anticipate what the trial testimony will be. Part of your trial prep is to anticipate as best you can which witnesses are most likely to "flip" on you when they testify. You should really have a good idea which prior inconsistent statements you might have to prove up using 725 ILCS 5/115-10.1.

You'll know which statements have been recorded or written down.

You may have some kind of grand jury transcripts or prior trial transcripts from a witness. These are the witnesses you can prepare for and can anticipate what to do when the witness begins "to come off" the prior statement. Thinking about this issue beforehand goes a long way. You'll always know what prior inconsistent statements can be proven as substantive evidence at trial.

It's also helpful to think about what "oral statements" exist in your discovery. You'll want to be aware of the witnesses who have made statements that were not recorded or written down. You'll likely have a few witnesses you wish were on paper or were recorded.

You'll want to ask yourself what might these witnesses say at trial? Maybe they will recant. Maybe they'll get on the stand

and say,

"I don't know."

Maybe the witness asserts some kind of privilege. You should be thinking about all this. Once you do, you'll realize there is no way to substantively prove these statements. This is when you should start to think about filing a motion for an "acknowledgment hearing."

The gist of the motion is that you are requesting a hearing before the court where you call the witness you'd like to "lock-in." When the witness is on the stand, you ask them about the statement.

Specifically, you lay the foundation like you would for impeachment with prior inconsistent statements. You treat it like any other prior inconsistent statement. You run through the time, place, and circumstance of the statement and confront the witness with the statement.

You 3 C's it.

When you get to the "confrontation" part you just treat it like any other confrontation of a witness. You ask directed, very narrow questions that ask exactly what you believe the statement to be. If the witness acknowledges making the statement, then you are done. You've just had the witness acknowledge under oath that they made the statement.

At trial, if the witness says anything different, you'll be able to admit the prior inconsistent statement as substantive evidence.

In this example, we started with a victim of domestic violence. Likely, the prosecutor has a police officer as a witness who can testify that the victim was crying when he got there and told him her husband punched her in the face. If this statement is not written down or recorded, the witness can only be impeached with this testimony at trial. The statement is not coming in as substantive evidence if it is not written down or recorded.

But Do I Have To?

So you may be wondering,

"What's the point of running the acknowledgment hearing if the witness *may* admit to making the statement and the jury is still going to hear what she told the police?"

For the prosecution, the reason for the hearing is crucial. If they suspect the victim is going to recant at trial and they know they don't have a written or recorded statement from her, they will quickly realize there is a good chance they could rest their case without any substantive evidence against the defendant.

It's a risky gamble for them that the witness will admit the statement. She could just as easily deny making it.

The prosecution would want to run an acknowledgment hearing to "lock-in" the victim's oral statement to the police. That way, if she does recant at the trial they at least salvaged some substantive evidence from her oral statement to the police.

Likewise, one could easily imagine it is the defense who requests an acknowledgment hearing. If the defense is confident that the victim would not only recant but also deny making the oral statement you can imagine the defense would be quite eager to conduct the hearing.

If the victim denies making the statement during the hearing, then the prosecution could be stopped dead in its tracks at trial when they try to impeach her with the oral statement to the police.

In this case, if the victim recants and denies making the oral statement, the state truly has no evidence against the accused. The defendant's motion for a directed finding after the state's case in chief would likely be granted. The state's case can be cut out right from underneath them.

It is not uncommon in criminal cases to have witnesses who are cooperating *at the moment*. Criminal law attorneys understand that sometimes cooperation doesn't last forever. This can be true on either side.

The prosecution may have an eyewitness who is cooperating, but they fear he or she could "turn" in the near future. Similarly, the defense may be aware of an alibi witness who is cooperating. Maybe the alibi witness is in and out of drug rehab, and for the moment they are out. It's easy to imagine a party with a "shaky witness" rushing to court for an acknowledgment hearing.

This way, the party who is aware of favorable statements can serve to lock them in before the witness changes their mind. If the witness has acknowledged making the statement in an acknowledgment hearing and they do change their mind, it doesn't matter.

This is very similar to the common practice of putting cooperating gang witnesses in front of a grand jury. The grand jury testimony serves to lock-in the gang witness testimony. At trial, when the witness suddenly remembers he hates the police and refuses to answer questions, it won't matter. The grand jury testimony comes in as substantive evidence.

Additionally, *Brothers* encourages attorneys to litigate these scenarios in a pretrial hearing before the trial. The trial is the last place to test if the witness is going to stick to his or her earlier statement. Squeezing a witness for the reason why they "can't remember" is risky when you do it in front of the jury.

If you as an attorney are aware of a statement that is not written down or recorded, and you don't have transcripts from a prior hearing or trial, this is when you should be thinking of an acknowledgment hearing.

It's true that the statute allows a witness to acknowledge a prior statement during the trial. You are not necessarily required to conduct a pretrial hearing. Every attorney has to decide when it's best to conduct the hearing. *Brothers* encourages us to consider a pretrial acknowledgment hearing in cases when you think you may have a particularly hostile or uncooperative witness.

As a rule of thumb, you should consider questioning messy or particularly uncooperative witnesses outside the presence of the jury.

The Danger Is Real

The danger courts have traditionally had with out-of-court statements is that limited-purpose impeachment testimony is often confused with substantive evidence.

As we can see in the case law, it is extremely confusing to the jury and even to us practitioners to determine exactly how testimony is being used. The assumption is that if something was said in court, it must be evidence.

We know that isn't always true. You don't have to search too long to find example after example where one party gets carried away with "impeachment only" testimony that is treated as substantive evidence.

Impeachment-only statements were given that label because they were thought of as unreliable and untrustworthy. There's no prior opportunity to cross-examine on these statements. With an impeachment-only statement, the opposing side doesn't have a chance to challenge the making of the statement. This is why judges didn't want these statements being treated as substantive evidence.

You have to remember why we have all these rules and procedures. The danger is real.

THE ACKNOWLEDGMENT HEARING

There are two opposing principles at work. Prior to the statute there was a strict rule that only allowed hearsay for impeachment. Out-of-court statements generally could not be used as substantive evidence. The statute is a compromise because it allows a party, usually the state, to basically get around an uncooperative witness who is not consistent in their testimony.

Now, attorneys can use the statute to get around troublesome testimony.

The compromise is that the statement needs to be recorded, written down and signed, or made in a prior trial so we all know it was definitely made. If we can establish with a high degree of certainty that the statement was made, then we are allowed not only to impeach the witness with the statement but also use the statement as evidence.

By having an acknowledgment hearing you get to test a previously "impeachment only" statement. Away from the jury there is no risk of improper information bleeding before the jury. If the "test" is passed, you then get to treat the statement as substantive evidence.

This is huge.

And there is no real reason why attorneys should not make more use of acknowledgment hearings. After an acknowledgment by a witness that they made the statement there is no more confusion or uncertainty about the statement.

If the acknowledgment is made during a pretrial hearing,

everyone is going to know with high certainty that the prior inconsistent statement can properly be treated as substantive evidentiary.

Judges Too

Judges should also see value in conducting an acknowledgment hearing before the actual trial.

However, some judges may not see the point. They may prefer to just play the case out during the trial and allow the witness to acknowledge or not acknowledge right there on the stand before the jury. A judge may not want to "waste time" before trial.

This is where the *Brothers* case would have to be cited and argued to the court.

Steigmann says this is a good idea. There are good practical reasons to run the motion. The arguments discussed above should be raised if you're confronted with a reluctant judge.

All of this is particularly relevant with a hostile or uncooperative witness. Let's reconsider our domestic violence example. Without an acknowledgment hearing it's easy to imagine how the trial would unfold.

Recall that in this example the victim tells the police at the scene that her husband punched her in the face. The statement was not recorded or written down. During the trial, she testifies that she was not hit and denies saying that to the police.

If there hasn't been an acknowledgment hearing, the prosecutor is going to want to explore the prior statement with the witness on the stand, right there in front of the jury. You can't fault the prosecution for that. No party is likely to just accept recantation testimony without trying to explore why that is happening.

Invariably, an attorney dealing with a recanting witness is going to explore the setting of the prior statement and really dig into it with the witness.

The jury is taking it all in the whole time.

The jury might be instructed that the witness' prior statement can only be considered for impeachment. We know that might not matter. The prosecution likely would have scored some points in front of the jury just for asking the questions. The problem is that if the victim continues to deny the statement it can't be used as substantive evidence.

...and you never really know which witnesses are going to deny it and which ones are going to admit it.

There has to be a limit as to how much the jury can or should hear about the prior inconsistent statement. It's natural and understandable for the prosecution to root out and explore why the victim is making a different statement. This means the substance of the prior statement is going to spill over into the jury's ears. The point of *Brothers* is to remind us that this *should happen*. But until we are confident the witness will acknowledge the statement, this back-and-forth with a witness *should happen outside the presence of the jury.*

Closing Thoughts

Clearly, this issue comes up much more frequently for the state.

The defense is also served well by knowing the "ins" and "outs" of the issue. However, the rule doesn't say that only the prosecution can avail itself of it.

The defense is free to use it to "lock-in" favorable witnesses just as freely as the prosecution can. Prosecutors can always turn to grand jury testimony to accomplish the same thing. Defense attorneys don't exactly have that opportunity.

A defense attorney can rely on an acknowledgment hearing. If you have a witness who is likely to recant by the time trial comes along, it's going to be in your interest to "lock-in" the testimony before the trial comes around.

Without a doubt, the state uses 725 ILCS 5/ 115-10.1 more often than the defense. However, the defense is served well by knowing when impeachment and the statute are being used correctly and when they are not.

The defense has to know what to be on guard for and know exactly when testimony is coming in for impeachment only and when it has substantive value. This way, practitioners will be able to identify when testimony is being used for the wrong purpose.

One should really read the *Brothers* case.

It talks about all kinds of scenarios that can happen in a trial like the "recanting recanter" or the "double turncoat" witness. At the end of the day, witnesses are people, and people are strange and unpredictable. You may get a witness who acknowledges making a statement outside the presence of the jury. Then when the jury is brought in, said witness may change their testimony.

Brothers contemplates all this.

Basically, it doesn't matter what the witness does in front of the jury. If the witness acknowledges the statement, it's coming in as evidence. An acknowledged statement can be treated like a recorded statement. By having the hearing, you've now created substantive evidence under 725 ILCS 5/115-10.1 right out of thin air.

With a recanting-recanter, you just react calmly and cooly as you start pulling up transcripts from the acknowledgment hearing. Yes, you start impeaching them with their testimony from the acknowledgment hearing, that's the whole point.

That's allowed because it's now substantive evidence.

Everything goes back to the question,

> *"Can this prior statement be proven substantively?"*

The acknowledgment hearing helps us answer this for especially troublesome witnesses.

9

57 Pages And Five Examples Of "How To Do It"

In this chapter we'll walk through 5 examples that demonstrate how a prior inconsistent statement can come up at trial. We'll focus on what the correct response from the attorney conducting the examination should be.

The Reckless Homicide Impeaching Witness Example

We'll begin with a DUI reckless homicide case. Let's say the accused drunk driver was in a black car and the victim driver was in a white car. Let's also assume that there was a witness to the accident. The witness originally told the police the white car had the green light.

At the trial the witness to the accident testifies and says,

"I saw the accident, and the black car had the green light."

That's a problem for the prosecution. They have a prior inconsistent statement from the witness saying otherwise. They have an interview this witness did with a police officer where the officer asks the witness,

Q: "Did you see this accident?"

Witness says,

A: "Yes, I did."

Q: "What did you see?"

A: "I'm not sure who had the green light. It might have been the white car."

This is a fairly simple situation.

You want to impeach this witness with their prior inconsistent statement. People don't understand how you are supposed to do this. You have to lay the proper foundation. Illinois Rule of Evidence 613 lays it out. This is what you had to do in the past.

Now it is all written down.

It says, "Extrinsic Evidence of Prior Inconsistent Statement of Witness," part (b),

> "Extrinsic evidence of a prior inconsistent statement by a witness is not admissible unless the witness is first afforded an opportunity to explain or deny the same

and the opposing party is afforded an opportunity to interrogate the witness thereon..."

Now what does that mean?

It tells us what we have to do when the witness is saying something different than they've said before. You roll right into the impeachment questions. Like this,

Q: "Did you say the WHITE car had the green light?"

A: "I'm not sure. I think it was the black car."

Q: "Mr. Smith, directing your attention to September 23, 2018 around 2:45 p.m., at that time you were walking your dog near the intersection of Maple and Union Streets in Aurora, Illinois?"

A: "Yes, I was there."

Q: "At that time and place did you have an opportunity to talk to an officer who responded to the accident you observed?"

A: "Yes, I did."

Q: "Did you have the occasion to talk to Officer McNulty at the scene of the accident?"

A: "Yes, I did."

Q: "And did Officer McNulty ask you what you saw?"

A: "Yes, he did."

Q: "And did you tell Officer McNulty that you weren't sure which car had the green light, but you thought that the white car may have had it?"

At this point the witness decides how to respond. He either says "yes" or "no." If he says "yes," then you've completed your impeachment. If he says, "No, I don't remember" or anything short of "yes," you must complete the impeachment by presenting extrinsic evidence that the prior statement was said.

One of the reasons for this is fairness to the witness and fairness to opposing counsel. If he admits to making the original statement, opposing counsel can get up there on redirect or cross and ask the witness to explain why he made the original statement.

Opposing counsel could simply ask,

Q: "Well, why did you think the white car had the green light?"

The witness may say,

A: "Well, I was confused. I was in the heat of the moment. When I got home I was thinking about it more carefully, and I realized that I was wrong."

Opposing counsel always has the chance to ask the witness to come up with some sort of explanation for the earlier statement.

The witness could also go the other way with this. If the impeaching attorney asks the witness,

Q: "Do you remember this conversation?"

The witness could also answer this way,

A: "No, I don't remember saying anything like that. Sure, I remember talking to the officer. I explained everything that happened. But I don't remember saying anything like what you just said."

Okay. Now what happens?

Having already laid the proper foundation, the party that impeached the witness must call the impeaching witness, but here's where problems often come in.

Things begin normal enough when Officer McNulty takes the stand. You have to begin by laying the proper foundation again with the officer. You ask,

Q: "Officer McNulty, did you have occasion to speak with this witness, and did you ask him what he saw?"

A: "Yes, I did."

Typically, lawyers then ask,

Q: "What did he say?"

And that's improper. That is wrong. If opposing counsel is alert, astute, and aware, they can shut you down faster than a teenage beer party gets shut down on prom night. You have to lead the witness. Only direct, limited, and leading questions will do here. That's the right way to do it. You have to ask this way,

Q: "Did he tell you at that time that he wasn't sure which car had the green light, but he believes it was the white car?"

That is a "yes" or "no" question. Nothing else will do here.

When you are preparing the impeaching witness, in this case Officer McNulty, he understands it's a "yes" or "no" answer. It's a leading question.

When he answers "yes," you are done.

Lawyers constantly forget to lay the proper foundation to begin with, and then when they call the impeaching witness they ask an open-ended question. Asking the impeaching witness,

"What did he say?"

That has no place in a trial. The impeaching witness has no competency other than to complete the impeachment. That's their only job and their only role. The officer was not there. He is not an occurrence witness. He doesn't know. All he knows is what he was told.

The impeaching witness is not there to testify about the details of the crime. It's not an open-ended question he is receiving.

You are just eliciting extrinsic evidence of the prior statement the witness denied making.

If an attorney were proceeding under 725 IlCS 5/115-10.1, it would work the same way. The statute was built upon the pre-existing foundation on how to impeach a witness. Whether you are proceeding under the statute or classical impeachment, it doesn't matter, you do the same thing.

You have to lay the proper foundation to impeach a witness with a prior inconsistent statement. Once that is done you can confront the witness with the statement. If the witness admits to making the statement, you are done, you have just perfected the impeachment. If the witness denies making the statement you are obligated to perfect the impeachment by calling the impeaching witness to answer direct and leading questions about the statement.

The Granny Acknowledgment Hearing Example

Let's consider another example that helps illustrate an acknowledgment hearing.

In this example we have a defendant accused of a brutal murder. The victim was discovered bleeding with mud on her clothing. Two hours later the police went to the suspect's residence and see his grandmother there. The suspect isn't there. But the grandmother tells the police that,

"Yes, my grandson, Chris, came home last night around 12:30, and he had mud and blood on his clothes. For the first time in his life, he did his own laundry shortly after getting home."

That's the kind of evidence prosecutors usually want the jury to know about. Prosecutors begin to salivate just thinking about letting the jury know that night was the first time in his life he decided to do his own laundry!

In this example you can see that almost anyone can develop a reason to change their testimony. This witness is a nice, law-abiding senior citizen. It's hard to imagine she would purposefully lie under oath.

Nonetheless, as the case develops and she sees exactly the kind of trouble her grandson is in, it causes her to either consciously or subconsciously reevaluate what she remembers.

On the stand, at the defendant's trial, Grandma testifies and says,

"I don't remember the night in question."

Under classical impeachment you can see how the prosecutor would be extremely frustrated. Here, we have a prosecutor who knows for sure that Grandma has some valuable information the jury should know.

Yet if Grandma changes her story by the time the trial came along, there was nothing the prosecutor could do about it. Trials were supposed to promote truth-seeking, yet the rule was preventing the very thing it purported to support.

At this point in the trial and under the modern rules, the attorney's reaction should be automatic. Alarm bells in their head are flashing and going off like a red alert fire. They know what Grandma should have said. Inconsistent trial testimony is instantly detected.

The 3 C's kick in…

Q: "Excuse me, ma'am, did you say you DO remember what happened that night?"

A: "No. I don't remember what happened."

Grandma just committed to her original testimony.

Q: "Do you remember how this whole thing started?"

A: "What do you mean?"

Q: "Well, you remember when the police came to your house late in the night on September 23, 2018?"

A: "Well, yes. I remember when they stopped by."

Q: "That hardly ever happens, am I right?"

A: "I'm friendly with the police, but they don't regular stop by like that."

Q: "Of course, and that night it was really late, after midnight, wasn't it around 2:30 am?"

A: "It was pretty late, I was already in my nightgown. I had locked everything down and around 2:30 little Rosie—Rosie, she's my poodle, and the light of my life—she started barking and making such a fuss. That's when I heard the knocking at the door. At first, I didn't want to answer. I just wanted them to go away. I was a little scared, I guess, 'cause I don't get visitors like that at night. Anyways, I could see through the window, it was the police. So I felt better, and I went to let them in."

Q: "You spoke with Detective McNulty, you remember that?"

A: "That sounds right."

Q: "This happened over at your place on Maple Street, 123 Maple Street in Aurora is that right?"

A: "Yes, they came to my house. That's where I live."

Q: "You and the police talked there for a little bit, didn't you?"

A: "Sure, they came in with all kinds of questions."

Q: "And you spoke to them, and you answered their questions?"

A: "I did. But I don't remember everything we talked about."

At this point, Grandma has committed to the statement and confirmed its details. Either way, she was set up and primed to be confronted with the prior inconsistent statement.

You have to keep it tight and leading. Use more than one question to make sure you get every single important detail. Track the exact language of the statement as you know it to be.

You say,

Q: "At that time, didn't you tell the police that, 'Chris came home last night around 12:30?'"

Notice I didn't indicate if the statement was recorded or not. Let's assume the statement was not recorded, nor written down, nor was Grandma put in front of a grand jury with her testimony.

Other than the detective's testimony there is no extrinsic evidence that she said it. This might be a prudent case for an acknowledgment hearing. Let's say the prosecutor tells the judge,

> "Judge, in good faith we believe that Grandma made certain statements to the police and she is not going to testify to that effect, so we want to conduct an acknowledgment hearing under 725 ILCS 5/115-10.1(c)(2)(b) of the statute and put Grandma on the witness stand. We want to conduct a hearing to confirm that Grandma, under oath on the witness stand out of the presence of the jury, acknowledges her prior statement to the police."

Let's assume you had this discussion before Grandma got on the bench, and the judge allows a short acknowledgment hearing away from the presence of the jury.

You'd begin exactly like we started this line of questioning. Then you ask,

Q: "At that time didn't you tell the police that, 'Chris came home last night around 12:30?'"

Grandma may say,

A: "Yes. I might have mentioned that."

In that case, Grandma has just acknowledged the statement as to that point, but you have to keep going with all the important points of the statement.

Q: "At that time didn't you tell the police that when Chris came home, 'he had mud and blood on his clothes?'"

A: "Yes. I remember that, but honestly I didn't get a good look, and I don't know for sure if Chris had blood on his clothes."

You're on a roll at this point, and there's one more question, there's that last little point about the laundry you're dying for the jury to know.

Q: "At that time didn't you tell the police that 'for the first time in his life he did his own laundry shortly after getting home?'"

A: "Well, I don't remember it like that."

Q: "But did you say that to the police?"

A: "No. I don't think I did."

Grandma didn't give it to you, but at this point, as a prosecutor, you'd be feeling pretty good. Grandma has just acknowledged making two out of three significant points in her prior statement. That means the prosecutor can argue to the jury that the accused got home around 12:30 a.m. the morning of the murder and had blood and mud on his clothes.

That's something.

Had the statement been recorded, the entire statement could have been used substantively as evidence. It wouldn't have mattered what Grandma said as long as she said something.

People might say,

"What's the point of clearing the jury and running an acknowledgment hearing?"

Grandma is going to say what she's going to say. Why clear the jury? But you never know what people may or may not say. Grandma might not think she is "testifying" when the jury is not there.

You just don't know what a witness will say until you ask the questions. Grandma might not think that it "counts" when the jury is gone. But we know it does count. Parts of Grandma's statement have just been converted to substantive evidence.

What if Grandma went all in on her bad memory? What if she

had denied making any part of the statement? Well then at least we know. And the reason for her sudden change in memory can be explored without tainting the jury with inadmissible evidence.

The prosecution has a clear line they can't cross at closing, and the defense has a clear standard they can enforce. Clear lines are good for everybody.

At this point it's just a matter of bringing the jury back in and asking Grandma about the statement in the presence of the jury.

If she says,

"Yes, I did tell the police that, but I was mistaken."

You have just completed the impeachment and it may now be considered and weighed by the jury.

If Grandma denies making the statement at all, then you know the prior statement can only be used for impeachment and everybody has to be very careful with exactly how they proceed.

If you are proceeding strictly under impeachment, as though Grandma has denied making the statement, you then have to follow through with the perfection of impeachment by calling Detective McNulty. That would go like this,

Q: "Detective McNulty, did you arrive at 123 Maple Street in Aurora around 2:20 a.m. on September the 23, 2018?"

A: "Yes, I did."

Q: Did you talk to the defendant's grandmother at that time?"

A: "Yes."

Q: "At that place and time did she tell you that her 'grandson, Chris came home last night around 12:30?'"

A: "Yes. She told me."

Q: "At that place and time did she tell you that when Chris came home 'he had mud and blood on his clothes?'"

A: "Yes. That's what she said."

Q: "At that place and time did she tell you that Chris, 'for the first time in his life he did his own laundry shortly after getting home?'"

A: "Yes, she did."

At this point, the impeachment has been perfected.

Under our example, the substance of the prior statement cannot be argued substantively. It can only be used to argue that Grandma can't be believed.

You can really see how things could have been different for the prosecution. Had the police written the statement out and then had Grandma sign it, or if they had recorded the conversation, it would have been better for the prosecution's case.

If that were the case as long as Grandma was in the box under oath and available for cross-examination, the entire prior statement would be coming in as evidence. With a written or recorded statement, it doesn't matter what Grandma says on the stand.

She could say,

> "Yeah, I made the statement, but that's what the cops told me to say. I was high on reefer and Jack Daniels. It doesn't matter. I didn't see anything. I just made it up. The cops put words in my mouth. I was scared and intimidated by them. They told me they'd take my little dog, Rosie, to the pound if I didn't say those things."

That's the type of stuff a witness is likely to say, and here's the thing, it doesn't matter. If you have paper or tape on the witness, none of that matters.

As long as she testifies about anything as opposed to just refusing to testify at all, which is another issue in itself, the prior inconsistent statement is admissible. The jury may consider it substantively as they decide whether or not the defendant is guilty.

That's the power of the statute and the modern rules.

My Brother Didn't Do It Example

The facts in this case are similar to a real life example from the case law. Here are the facts:

The charge is aggravated battery. The defendant is accused of choking a girl. The girl turns out to be best friends with the defendant's sister. There was an argument at the house when the friend was visiting.

Defendant grabs the girl's phone and runs away with it. The victim chases him, in part to get her phone back. She catches up to him and there is a physical confrontation. That's when the defendant puts his hands on her neck and chokes her. The defendant's sister gets in between them and breaks it up before it escalates even further.

The sister tells police at the scene words to the effect,

"My brother choked my friend, but I broke it up before it got too ugly. Thanks so much for showing up and helping me calm things down."

This statement is not recorded or written down.

This fact pattern was taken from a real-life example. The case is *People v. Lewis*, 2017 IL App (4th) 150124 (April), and it was authored by our friend Judge Steigmann.

There is a lot going on in this case, and it's a practical "how-to" lesson on how to conduct proper impeachment in an Illinois criminal courtroom. In the next chapter, you'll find some resources that include a copy of this case. This is one of the cases that should be read on this topic.

If you watch enough trials, no doubt you'll see a scene where an attorney can't get a piece of evidence admitted. Usually there is an objection. The attorney says something to overcome the objection. The judge sustains it. The attorney then tries again.

Objection sustained again.

Usually the attorney rephrases the same point they were making earlier. You can always tell when the attorney doesn't understand what error they are making. The judge begins to get annoyed and sustains the objection again.

Eventually, the attorney gives up and moves on to another question or sits down altogether out of frustration. This kind of situation is painful to watch. It hurts even more to experience it. Yet this kind of thing happens all the time. The *Lewis* case will go a long way toward ensuring that you are never the attorney who sits down.

Okay. I had to get that out of my system.

Let's get back to our example. What do you think happened at trial?

Of course, the sister gets on the stand to testify that there was no choking. She admits to some angry words and to some hostility, but she denies that her brother ever choked the victim.

It's the prosecution that now wants to impeach the sister with her prior inconsistent statement. It's the prosecution that wants the jury to know that at the time of the incident she told the police that her brother choked her friend. They want the jury to know this so that the jury doesn't believe her testimony in court.

First and foremost, this is just a pure impeachment question.

This is not a prior inconsistent statement under the statute (725 ILCS 5/115-10.1) because the statement is not written down, recorded nor does the witness affirm her statement. It's not coming in for substantive evidence. So it's purely impeachment.

The prosecution can only use the statement to attack the sister's truthfulness at trial.

The sister was actually called by the defendant and the prosecution on cross examination is looking to cancel out her testimony.

The problem for the state was the way the whole thing went down. To move things along, let's assume the prosecutor was able to get the witness to commit to her statement, and was able to confirm the time, place, and location of the statement. Then, in the state's cross-examination, the state asked the sister the following question,

Q: "Do you remember telling the officer that the defendant, choked your friend?"

The sister responded,

A: "No, I don't remember that."

The state is obligated at this point to perfect the impeachment. That means they have to prove up that in fact she did make the statement.

So the officer gets on the stand. He's the impeaching witness.

The state asks the officer,

Q: "Do you remember the interview with the defendant's sister?"

The officer says,

A: "Yes, of course I do."

Then the state asks,

Q: "Could you please begin at the beginning?"

At this point, you can imagine Judge Steigmann standing up, reading the transcripts, and completely losing his shirt. I imagine the trial transcripts were thrown to the grown and the judge probably stomped on them once or twice.

No. No. No. That is not how you do it. That is 100% wrong. That is not how you perfect impeachment.

57 PAGES AND FIVE EXAMPLES OF "HOW TO DO IT"

What's the problem?

We'll get into that.

First take note of what's happening in this case. The officer, with an open-ended question like that, begins to get into all kinds of statements and details that none of the witnesses talked about.

He's testifying to hearsay. What the sister told him is hearsay, plain and simple. The officer continues by testifying that,

> "Well, when I got there the defendant's sister told me there was a fight between her brother and her friend. At some point, her brother reached past the victim and grabbed her twice around the neck."

Steigmann has already lost his shirt and has stomped on the transcripts. Now you can picture him losing his crap and spitting on the transcripts. Zero impeachment perfection has happened. The officer is basically testifying to inadmissible hearsay.

The officer never confirms that the sister told him that her brother had choked the victim. That's why he was called to the stand in the first place. He never even uses the word "choked."

He said from the stand that,

"she told me that he grabbed her." What is that?

When an officer is asked to start at the beginning he or she will invariably get into inadmissible testimony. Right then and there at that moment opposing counsel needed to spit her water out, jump up off the chair and "object."

The objection should have been that,

"This is hearsay, your Honor. The witness has not perfected any impeachment at all."

In Steigmann's eyes this is supposed to be super simple and it gets completely fouled up.

"Wrong. Wrong. Wrong. Wrong."

Steigmann would have been yelling at us.

Steigmann lays it out the way it should have happened.

"This impeachment should have been perfected like this," he writes,

> *"Before a witness may be impeached by a prior statement, a proper foundation must be laid in order to alert the witness, avoid unfair surprise, and to give the witness a chance to explain. The witness must first be asked as to the time, place, and persons involved in the alleged conversation; secondly, he must be asked whether he made a certain contrary statement at that time... When the impeaching witness is produced, the proper course*

> *is simply to ask him whether or not the witness to be impeached made the statement in regard to which he has been questioned at that time and place mentioned. It is improper to ask the impeaching witness to relate the whole conversation."*

People v. Lewis, 2017 IL App (4th) 150124 (April), ¶ 53, quoting *People v. Ellis*, 41 Ill. App. 3d 377, 385, 354 N.E.2d 369, 385 (1976).

This is the 3 C's plain and simple, just the way we have already talked about.

When the impeaching witness is produced, in this case the officer, you must only and simply ask him whether the witness being impeached made the statement at that place and time in question.

This is 100% a leading question.

It's a "yes" or "no" response only. There is no wiggle room for anything else. It is improper to ask the impeaching witness to relate the whole conversation.

You can't ask the cop,

"What did the defendant's sister tell you?"

No. This is an open-ended question and therefore improper.

The proper way to ask the question would have been something like this,

Q: "You responded to the scene at 123 Mains Street, on January 23, 2018?"

A: "Yes."

Q: "You spoke to the defendant's sister at that time about what had happened?"

A: "Yes."

Q: "During that conversation, did the defendant's sister tell you that the defendant choked her friend, the victim, twice?"

A: "Yes."

And you are done.

This is how impeachment is perfected with an impeaching witness. Anything else is simply improper and inadmissible.

Why is this the rule?

Why is this the way it should be done? This case demonstrates exactly why. When you get sloppy with the questions, first of all, you run the risk of not even perfecting your impeachment. The witness may get lucky and say the things that need to be said. More likely, they will not.

Second, when you start using open-ended questions with an

impeaching witness you are asking for trouble. The impeaching witness is practically guaranteed to testify about and bring in all kinds of inadmissible hearsay and improper testimony.

This is why you can't ask an impeaching witness to tell us everything they know.

The information from an open-ended question may be, strictly speaking, relevant; but it also likely will have nothing to do with impeaching the earlier witness. The sole reason for calling an impeaching witness is to perfect the impeachment of the earlier witness.

That is why they were put on the stand and, for all intents and purposes, that is their sole reason for existence.

Without controlled, leading questions you'll likely get into prejudicial testimony as well. At that point, your case is going to sink faster than the Titanic near an iceberg.

This rule evolved before the substantive evidence changes in 725 ILCS 5/115-10.1. Before the statute none of this stuff was suppose to be admissible. The reason they clamped down and became real specific with the impeachment perfection was precisely to control what the jury hears.

If the prior statement was not substantive they didn't want the jury hearing anything else unrelated to the exact words the witness is believed to have said because there was always the risk the jury would treat substantively everything they heard.

That is a big, substantial, and real risk.

This is why short and narrow-to-the-point leading questions are the only way to conduct proper perfection of impeachment.

In case things have been less than clear, the main takeaway from the case is that:

> *Leading questions is the only proper way to conduct impeachment. That is true when you are confronting the witness who made the prior inconsistent statement, and it is also true with the impeaching witnesses you may call to perfect the impeachment.*

At the risk of dragging this out and being redundant, let's run through how the questioning of the defendant's sister should have gone down. We'll begin right when the sister says there was no choking.

The 3 C's have to kick in, and this is how the prosecutor continues questioning her:

Prosecutor first needs to confirm the statement.

Q: "Is it your testimony that your brother *CHOKED* your friend?"

Sister now has a chance to fix her mistake. Instead she confirms her statement. She says,

A: "No. It's not. I just said there was no choking. My brother didn't choke nobody."

Check.

The prosecutor now moves on to the 2nd C.

The prosecutor must confirm the statement, which means giving the witness a heads-up as to the time, place, location, and circumstance of the statement.

Q: "Well, isn't it true that on December 12, at around 8:35 p.m. police were called to your home at 123 Mains Street in Peoria, Illinois?"

A: "Yeah, so what?"

Q: "Police actually arrived correct?"

A: "Yes, they did."

Q: "That was the day your brother was arrested?"

A: "Yes. They took him."

Q: "Your friend, Suzy, was also there at that time?"

A: "Yeah, she was there."

Q: "You know Suzy from school, right?"

A: "Yeah, we at school together."

Q: "She's your friend, not your brother's friend?"

A: "Yeah, I guess."

Q: "Your friend was emotional and crying when the police got there, correct?"

A: "She wasn't emotional."

Q: "Ok, she was upset when the police got there?"

A: "Yeah, she was pissed."

Q: "She was angry?"

A: "Well, yeah."

Q: "She was mad?"

A: "Livid."

Q: "At you?"

A: "I didn't do nothing."

Q: "She was mad at your brother?"

A: "Of course, they got into it and yelling at each other."

Q: "Did your friend get arrested that night?"

A: "No. They only took my brother."

Q: "The police helped settle things down, correct?"

A: "We were already cooling off."

Q: "The police started asking questions?"

A: "They were doing a lot of things. I wasn't in their business."

Q: "Yeah, but you talked to them that night, correct?"

A: "Sure, they wanted to know what happened."

Q: "That's when you made a statement to the police about the incident that involved your brother and Suzy?"

A: "I guess. Yeah, I talked to them."

In this example, I really dragged this out. After this line of questioning it was clear to the jury that the sister remembers quite well what happened the night her brother was arrested.

This is overkill, but it's effective.

We got as far as the second C—check.

There is one more C to go. The attorney must now confront the witness with her prior statement to the police with nothing but the prior statement. They should be leading questions that quote the statement exactly.

You can break up the statement with a series of questions.

The witness confrontation would sound like this:

Q: "Didn't you tell the police officer that night that, 'my brother choked my friend?'"

You never really know what a witness will say, let's say, for example she replies,

A: "No way. Not true. I didn't tell 'em that."

You keep going...

Q: "Didn't you tell the police, 'my brother choked my friend but I broke it up before it got too ugly?'"

A: "Not even. I never said that."

You keep going...

Q: "Didn't you tell the police, 'Thanks so much for showing up and helping me calm things down?'"

A: "I didn't thank nobody for arresting my brother for nothing."

The truth is it doesn't matter how the sister answers the questions. If she admits to making the statements the impeachment is perfected, you can argue to the jury that her in-court testimony can't be believed.

If she actually acknowledges making the statement then the sister would have just complied with the "acknowledge" requirements of Section 725 ILCS 5/115-10.1(c)(2)(B), and the statement comes in as substantive evidence.

If she denies making the statement like in the example above, no problem. You just call the officer who talked to the sister that night, and he can perfect the impeachment. However, if she denies making the statement and you need to perfect impeachment with a witness, then you know the statement can only be used for impeachment.

That's it.

When the officer takes the stand, what you DON'T say to him is,

"Tell us what she told you."

Once the sister denies making the statement, the state is duty bound to perfect impeachment by calling the officer. If you want to get technical, we say the state must now perfect the impeachment by presenting extrinsic evidence of the prior inconsistent statement.

We did not harp on this, but if you cannot perfect impeachment with extrinsic evidence you've got no right to even ask the impeaching question in the first place. Why is that the rule?

For all the reasons we've talked about already. If you can't back it up an astute opposing counsel, maybe even the judge, won't allow you to expose the jury to testimony that is likely inadmissible as substantive evidence.

So if you can't back it up with extrinsic evidence, you can't get into it. In this example the officer is the extrinsic evidence, so the prosecution calls him to the stand.

Once the officer is on the stand here's how the questioning would go,

Q: "Officer, tell us your name?"

A: "I'm Officer McNulty. Badge number 253."

Q: "Do you work for the Peoria Police Department?

A: "Yes, I do."

Q: "Were you on duty on January 23, 2018?"

A: "Yes, I was."

Q: "Did you have the occasion to report to the location of 123 Mains Street in Peoria, Illinois, at around 8:35 p.m.?"

A: "Yes, I did."

Q: "At that place and time did you have a conversation with the defendant's sister about what had just transpired there?"

A: "Yes. I asked her a few questions."

Q: "During that conversation did the defendant's sister tell you that, 'my brother choked my friend?'"

It has to be this way. It has to be a leading question. Keep it tight and track the exact language of the statement. There can be no wiggle room for anything else. No open-ended questioning is being called for. This is a "yes" or "no" question. Nothing else.

In this case the officer should answer:

A: "Yes. That's what she said."

Q: "During that conversation did the defendant's sister tell you that, 'my brother choked my friend but I broke it up before it got too ugly?'"

A: "Yes. That's what she said."

Q: "During that conversation did the defendant's sister say to you, 'Thanks so much for showing up and helping me calm things down?'"

A: "That's how I recall it."

Part of the reason Steigmann was irked by this case was because after the officer is asked "to start at the beginning," he never really says what we all thought he was going to say. He never says defendant's sister told him her brother choked her friend.

When the officer finally got to the important part, he said the sister told him that her brother reached across and grabbed her by the neck. What the heck is that?

That was not exactly what the statement should have been. That just further muddied up the testimony. It was not perfecting the impeachment and instead it was just inadmissible hearsay.

In a real life setting the officer would have been prepped, and in that preparation for trial hopefully any inconsistencies would have been revealed. Indeed, during the trial preparation if the officer had said,

"You know, I think she told me that he grabbed her neck. She didn't say he choked her, she didn't say it like that."

Well okay, now a good faith basis exists for the state to ask about "grabbing." The prosecuting ASA must then act accordingly, not withstanding any discovery issues that may arise from the discrepancy.

This is a great example of why the rules exist and what can happen when you don't follow the rules as we know them. To sum it up, the State's open-ended questioning of the officer, the impeaching witness, had two bad results:

1. The State never properly completed the sister's impeachment because the officer never testified that the sister made the statement to him that was allegedly inconsistent with her trial testimony, and

2. The jury heard the officer testify to matters that were completely inadmissible hearsay. This was all relevant

information, but it was not part of the prior inconsistent statement.

Prosecutor Completely Loses Control Example

In this next example, we have two co-defendants charged with murder.

A gas station attendant was shot and killed during an armed robbery. Defendant and his co-defendant were seen exiting and fleeing from the gas station shortly after the shooting.

We'll call the defendant's co-defendant Larry. Larry has already been convicted in his own separate murder trial.

The state was aware that Larry had testified in his own trial and made some incriminating statements about himself and defendant. The state was well aware that Larry was planning on taking the Fifth if he were called to testify against this defendant. The state had anticipated this and granted him use immunity to prevent Larry from taking the Fifth.

Here's how Larry's direct examination went down:

(I'm going to include actual trial transcripts from the real case so you get a good idea of how this can transpire in real life.)

[Prosecutor] Q: "Would you state your name?"

A: "Deangelo, Larry."

Q: "And are you from the Peoria area?"

A: "Yes, ma'am."

Q: "Do you know a person by the name of Monica Loveless?"

A: "Yes, ma'am."

Q: "How do you know her?"

A: "It's my sister."

Q: "And back in May of 2009, did she live at 1207 West Main?"

A: "Yes, ma'am."

Q: "And were there times that you would frequent her apartment on Main?"

A: "Yeah."

Q: "I want to direct your attention to May 27th of 2009. Did you go into the USA Gas Station and attempt to commit an armed robbery?"

A: "I plead the Fifth."

[PROSECUTOR]: "Judge, I would—"

[THE COURT]: "I'm instructing you to answer that question."

[LARRY]: "I plead the Fifth."

[THE COURT]: "All right, I'm going to tell the jury this: Defendant has been given what we call use immunity, which means that nothing he says today in testimony can ever be used against him, and he's refusing to answer. He doesn't have the privilege to refuse to answer, so I'm ordering—"

[LARRY]: "So I can't not answer a question? That's what you all are saying?"

[THE COURT]: "Exactly. You're to answer."

[LARRY]: "So me as a human, I can't answer?"

[THE COURT]: I'm ordering you—

[DEFENSE ATTORNEY]: 'Your Honor, I will object at this point. He is asking for legal advice. His counsel is not here."

[THE COURT]: "Are you representing him?"

[DEFENSE ATTORNEY]: "I'm not representing him."

[THE COURT]: "I'm ordering you to answer the question."

[LARRY]: "I want to talk to my lawyer."

[THE COURT]: "Are you refusing to answer the questions?"

[LARRY]: "To any other questions, I plead the Fifth."

[PROSECUTOR]: Q: "You're currently in the Department of Corrections?"

A: "Yes, ma'am."

Q: "That's for first degree murder?"

A: "Accountability."

Q: "For first-degree murder?"

A: "Yes, ma'am."

Q: "Do you know a person by the name of Ali Evans?"

A: "Yes, ma'am."

Q: "And do you see the person you know as Ali Evans in court today?"

A: "Yes, ma'am."

Q: "Could you point him out and describe what he's wearing?"

A: "(Indicating) In a black suit, glasses, look real nice."

[PROSECUTOR]: "Judge, may the record reflect the witness identified the defendant?"

[THE COURT]: "Noted for the—"

Q: "And the judge informed you that you cannot do that and is ordering you to testify."

A: "Yes, ma'am."

Q: "So do you remember? Do you remember when the gas station clerk died? Let's start with the easy one. Do you remember that? That's a question."

A: "I plead the Fifth."

Q: "And you don't have that right. Yes or no, do you remember—yes or no, do you remember when the gas station clerk lost his life? Do you remember, yes or no?"

A: "I plead the Fifth."

Q: "Let's start with—let's start with another easy one. Do you remember the gun you used when the gas station clerk lost his life."

A: "I plead the Fifth."

Q: "Do you remember the gun you touched?"

A: "That's a question?"

Q: "Yes."

A: "I plead the Fifth."

Q: "Well, your fingerprints are on the gun."

A: "To my knowledge, it's not my trial. I got found guilty, remember?"

Q: "So you don't know if your fingerprints were on the gun?"

A: "I plead the Fifth."

Q: "You plead the Fifth?"

A: "Yes, ma'am."

Q: "You don't have that right. Were your fingerprints on the murder weapon?"

A: "I plead the Fifth."

Q: "Were your fingerprints on it because you grabbed the murder weapon from Ali Evans?"

A: "I plead the Fifth."

Q: "Were you at your sister's house or sister's apartment before you went over to the gas station?"

A: "I plead the Fifth."

Q: "You have to answer the question. Were you at your sister's apartment before you and Mr. Evans went to the gas station?"

A: "My answer is that I plead the Fifth."

Q: "Were you just chilling at your sister's crib before you went to the store? (No response.) Were you chilling at your sister's crib before you went to the store?"

A: "I'm not going to answer any more questions. I'm giving you all the same answer every time."

Q: "I know, and you can't use that answer."

A: "I'm wasting y'all time. You all got me up here."

Q: "It's a simple yes or no question."

[DEFENSE ATTORNEY]: "Your Honor, I'll object to further questioning."

[THE COURT]: "Why don't you approach."

(A bench conference was held.)

[PROSECUTOR]: Q: "On May 27th, 2009, when you and Mr. Evans went into the store and Mr. Evans was up in front of the cashier, did you tell him that 'there wasn't a gun? There was no gun, Bro?'"

A: "I plead the Fifth."

[DEFENSE ATTORNEY]: "Objection."

[THE COURT]: "Overruled."

[PROSECUTOR]: Q: "When the two of you went in the store, was the purpose to rob the store clerk, but that you were simply at that point going to see how many people were in the store."

A: "I plead the Fifth."

Q: "Or how many people are working?"

A: "I plead the Fifth."

Q: "Did you go through the middle aisle, and did Bro, being Mr. Evans, walk around the first aisle and say, 'Fuck this shit. Ain't nobody here,' and then go up to the cashier?"

[DEFENSE ATTORNEY]: "Objection."

A: "My answer is the last time I'm answering, I plead the Fifth."

[THE COURT]: "What's your objection?"

[DEFENSE ATTORNEY]: "This is just the prosecutor testifying at this point, Your Honor. He's told us very clearly he's not going to answer any more questions."

[THE COURT]: "He did answer some questions. I'm going to—but I will sustain it in the sense that we are getting to—I mean, it's leading, so—"

[PROSECUTOR]: "Could we approach on that?"

[THE COURT]: "Yes."

(A bench conference was held.)

[PROSECUTOR]: Q: "Did Ali Evans go up to the clerk and say, 'Give me that shit. Give me that shit?'"

[DEFENSE ATTORNEY]: "Objection."

[THE COURT]: "Sustained."

[PROSECUTOR]: Q: "What did Ali Evans say to the cashier?"

[DEFENSE ATTORNEY]: "Objection."

[THE COURT]: "Overruled."

[PROSECUTOR]: Q: "What did the cashier do?"

A: "I'm not answering any more questions. I'm pleading the Fifth."

Q: "Did the cashier bend down to reach for money?"

[DEFENSE ATTORNEY]: "Objection."

[LARRY]: "You all can't take me out of here?"

[THE COURT]: "Hold on. Overruled. To answer your question now—"

[LARRY]: "I'm not answering your questions. I plead the Fifth, sir."

[THE COURT]: "Okay."

[LARRY]: "I don't know nothing. I want to go back to where I belong in your eyes, and I'll leave it at that."

[PROSECUTOR]: Q: "Did the defendant shoot the cashier?"

[DEFENSE ATTORNEY]: "Objection."

[THE COURT]: "Overruled."

[PROSECUTOR]: Q: "Did Ali shoot the cashier? It's a yes or no question. Did Ali shoot the cashier? (No response.) Enjoy your life in prison."

[DEFENSE ATTORNEY]: "Objection, Your Honor."

[LARRY]: "Don't object. Don't object. She mean that, her exact meaning."

[PROSECUTOR]: "I have no further questions."

[THE COURT]: "Sustained. Disregard that last comment. [Counsel for defendant], do you want to ask any questions?"

[LARRY]: "Why disregard it? She meant it. This is the people that got us going to jail."

[THE COURT]: "All right. Take him out."

[LARRY]: "Good luck with your trial, Bro."

Here's the thing, Larry testified in his own trial. He was "under oath at a trial" which meant that prior testimony was admissible under 725 ILCS 5/115-10.1(c)(1).

The prosecution had paper on him and should have been ready to kick into the foundation questions.

Right at the beginning when Larry indicated he was not going to testify, he should have been asked,

Q: "I want to direct your attention to May 27th of 2009. Did you go into the USA Gas Station and attempt to commit an armed robbery?"

A: "I plead the Fifth."

Right there, the state had already litigated the fifth amendment issue and had a green light to proceed. Larry is basically refusing to answer any questions about the robbery. The prosecutor should have responded by asking,

[PROSECUTOR]: Q: "Are you saying you're prepared to testify here today about what happened at the USA Gas Station on May 27, 2009?"

[LARRY]: "That's not what I'm saying. I'm telling you I'm taking the Fifth."

Okay.

The prosecutor should have immediately moved to get Larry to confirm the time, date, location, and circumstances of his testimony.

The prosecutor has already given Larry a chance to get his act together. Instead, Larry chose to commit to his inconsistent trial testimony. Next, the prosecutor needs to move into stage two. It would sound like this,

[PROSECUTOR]: Q: "Diverting your attention to February 18, 2013, on that day did you testify under oath in a trial in this court building?"

[LARRY]: "Whatever, you know I did. You were there."

Q: "When you testified there was a court reporter present recording your testimony just like right now?"

A: "They was a lot of people there."

Q: "And in that trial did you testify about the events that happened at the USA Gas Station on May 27, 2009?"

A: "I'm not answering anymore."

Q: "At that trial did you testify about who you were with, where you were before going to the gas station and where you went after you left the gas station?"

A: "I'm done."

It's worth pointing out how the witness answers the questions doesn't really matter. The point is to give the witness a chance to acclimate themselves to the making of the statement.

The point is that we are getting ready to confront the witness with the prior inconsistent statement. Before we can do that we need to put up huge blinking road lights to let the witness know what's coming.

The witness doesn't need to acknowledge any of these questions. Second C, "confirm" questions have to be asked so the witness knows where the "confrontation" questions are coming from.

Don't get hung up if the witness continues to deny knowing about the time, date, location, and circumstances of the statement.

You just keep going.

At this point the foundation for confrontation has been laid. Rather than argue and get into it with Larry, the prosecutor should have just stuck to the script and continued with her proper questioning.

If there's an "objection," all the prosecutor has to do is explain to the court that she is impeaching the witness as the statute and the rules allow.

The "confrontation" questions would look like this,

[PROSECUTOR] Q: "When you testified in the trial on February 18, 2013 in this very courthouse, did you testify that, 'I ran into Ali, and we decided to get together later at my sister's house?'"

[LARRY]: "THE FIFTH."

Q: "Did you testify that, 'Ali talked about robbing his uncle and he showed me a gun?'"

A: "Nope. I'm not playing anymore."

Eventually, the prosecutor would get to the really important confrontation question.

Q: "Did you testify that, 'Ali just pointed the gun at the clerk guy and shot him when dude reached for something under the counter?'"

This is how it would go line by line, point by point, on every important point from the prior statement.

It doesn't matter how Larry answers. In this example, it just means the prosecutor needs to be ready to have the court reporter from Larry's trial take the stand to perfect his impeachment.

In a case like this, that would be a truly simple affair. It might sound like this:

[PROSECUTOR] Q: "Can you tell us your name and occupation?"

[COURT REPORTER] A: "I'm Julie Jane, and I'm a court reporter. I transcribe oral testimony given in this courthouse."

Q: "Did you transcribe testimony given under oath in this courthouse in Room 354 on February 18, 2018?"

A: "I did."

Q: "Did Larry DeAngelo testify in that trial and did you transcribe and record his testimony?"

A: "I did transcribe his testimony."

Q: "In that trial did Larry testify that, 'I ran into Ali, and we decided to get together later at my sister's house?'"

A: "Yes, he did."

Q: "In that trial did Larry testify that, 'Ali talked about robbing his uncle and he showed me a gun?'"

A: "Yes, he did."

All this questioning would be occurring with the aid of the trial transcripts. You just read directly from them to make sure you only track and trace the exact words spoken by Larry.

Q: "In that trial did Larry testify that, 'Ali just pointed the gun at the clerk guy and shot him when dude reached for something under the counter?'"

A: "Yes, that's how he testified."

This example was inspired by the real life case of *People v. Evans*, 2016 IL App (3d) 140120 (July). The actual transcripts at the top were pulled right from the court opinion. In the real case the prosecutor never asked the impeachment foundational questions and never perfected the impeachment with the court reporter.

What was the problem with the actual direct examination?

Well, the reviewing court said the prosecutor improperly disclosed the substance of Larry's alleged prior statement to the jury through leading or suggestive questions, which presumed facts not in evidence.

The result of Larry's refusal to answer questions about the murder was that the State was able to present its theory of the case without the defendant having the ability to cross-examine Larry on those matters.

The defense was deprived of meaningful cross-examination of Larry.

Simply stated, it was error for the trial court to allow the prosecutor to continue questioning Larry about all of the circumstances of the murder. The prosecutor essentially disclosed the substance of Larry's prior testimony without giving the defendant a chance to cross-examine Larry on the statement. The prosecutor's failure to abide by 725 ILCS 5/115-10.1, Rule 613(b) and Rule 801(d)(1)(A)(1) all lead to reversible error in the case.

If the proper foundation had been laid, Larry's prior trial testimony made under oath would have been admitted substantively as a prior inconsistent statement.

Immediately after Larry testified that he did not remember if he was with the defendant on the day of the murder, formal impeachment under the rules should have begun.

The problem was that no attempt was made to use the rules to put into evidence Larry's prior inconsistent statement. The fundamental problem was that the details of the crime came from the prosecutor's questions and not from Larry's prior statement.

How To Think Through A Problem

The focus in this last example is to analyze the thought process an attorney should run through when she or he is confronted with a prior inconsistent statement problem during a trial.

Say we have an aggravated DUI where the defendant was accused of huffing a can of compressed air when he blacked out, crashed, and rolled the car he was driving. Three male passengers in the back seat all were killed while the defendant and the front seat passenger survived.

The front seat passenger (Frizzy) tells the police at the hospital that,

> *"I was looking out the window listening to some music that was playing and then Jim asked me a question so I started talking to him, and that's when I turned around, and you know, looking at the backseat...started talking to Jim, and I can't remember if it was Ben or Ken that said, 'Hey Morgan, you shouldn't be doing that.'"*

Frizzy's interview at the hospital was recorded on a small digital audio recorder. Despite the death of three of his friends, Frizzy is still friends with the defendant and doesn't want to see him get in any more trouble over the accident.

In defendant's trial the state calls Frizzy to the stand, and he testifies, in part that,

> *"I was in the process of thinking of a way to convince my mom to let me out of school the next day because we had a half a day, so I was busy on my phone, and a little bit before, Jim had asked me what we were going to do when we got back, and I said I thought we were going over–we were going to go over to one of my friend's house, and he said 'yeah, that's fine,' and we didn't talk after that. And then we just kept riding. The music was on. It was fine. And then they kept saying his name over and over again. And I wasn't sure what was happening, so I looked back,*

> *and they were all—they all—their attentions were focused on him, trying to wake him up. I'm not sure what had happened."*

In the trial it becomes obvious that the prosecution is laying the foundation to impeach Frizzy with the recorded interview from the hospital.

It's clear to both sides what is missing. Frizzy keeps out the part where one of the boys from the back seat says to defendant,

"Hey Morgan, you shouldn't be doing that."

The prosecution wants to argue to the jury that the defendant was seen huffing from the can and that the back seat passengers were trying to discourage him from doing that.

The defense attorney stands up and "objects," and then asks the judge for a few moments to gather her thoughts. The judge says,

"Take all the time that you need."

So, can the defense attorney keep that recorded statement out? Or is it coming in? What should counsel tell the judge?

To begin with, the defense attorney quickly runs through the threshold questions.

- Is the in-court testimony inconsistent with the hospital's recorded statement? If there is an inconsistency here, it's inconsistent by omission, but that counts. Counsel shouldn't bet she can convince the court that the statement is not inconsistent. **It is, indeed, inconsistent.**

- Next threshold question. Is the prior inconsistent statement material? Hell yeah. Was the kid taking a puff from a can right before the crash? **Yes. That's material.** Can't dwell on that here. Must move on with the analysis.

Now we quickly need to "rule in" or "rule out" if Frizzy's recorded hospital statement meets the other elements of 725 ILCS 5/115-10.1.

- Can it come in under the statute as substantive evidence?

- Let's see, was the prior statement made under oath in a sworn statement? No. No way. Frizzy didn't testify about this in any other trial, proceeding, or hearing. The state didn't put him in front of a grand jury either, so no.

- Next question: Was the prior statement recorded? Bingo! They got tape on the kid at the hospital. **This statement was definitely recorded.** This looks like it could be a prior inconsistent statement under the statute.

But there is one quick last question that must be asked.

- Did Frizzy have personal knowledge of the contents of the statement? Frizzy said he heard a back seat passenger say to defendant, "Hey Morgan, you shouldn't be doing that."

Frizzy didn't say the statement. He heard someone in the back say it.

- Actually, Frizzy was distracted on his phone either texting his mom or listening to music or both. Frizzy was not paying attention to what the driver was doing. No way. **Frizzy has no personal knowledge of the contents of the statement.** Bingo! Happy lights are going off in the attorney's head because she knows what she is going to tell the judge.

But counsel can't be done asking questions because even if the state loses on substantive evidence, you can bet for darn sure they will try to impeach Frizzy with the statement for impeachment purposes only. This attorney would try that herself, so she's pretty sure the prosecutor will try that as well.

- Okay. Whose witness is this? This is the state's own witness. If defense counsel was trying to impeach him, it would be allowed, but this is the state's own witness so...

- Did this witness affirmatively damage the state's case? The state has to establish that the witness has affirmatively damaged their case if they want to impeach him with a prior inconsistent statement.

- If the state has just been disappointed, they can't impeach their own witness. The kid actually gave it all up. He just left out that one crucial part.

- But you know it's not like Frizzy is saying he saw the driver, and he didn't have an aerosol can in his hand. Frizzy is not saying he didn't see the driver huffing. He's not saying that. He's just saying they kept saying his name over and over, but he admits he doesn't know what was happening. **That's not affirmative damage.**

- The state is no worse off had they never called Frizzy to the stand. There is no affirmative damage here so they can't impeach the witness with the prior recorded inconsistent statement.

After the attorney has taken a few moments to run all these ideas through her head, she tells the judge,

"Judge, may we approach?"

Judge says, "Sure. Why not?"

At the bench away from the jury, she tells the judge,

> "Judge, it's pretty clear the state wants to confront this witness with his recorded hospital statement to the police, specifically the part where he tells them he heard a backseat passenger say 'Hey Morgan, you shouldn't be doing that.' Well judge, there is no rule of evidence that allows that. This is not a prior inconsistent statement under 725 ILCS 5/115-10.1 because although the statement is recorded, the declarant had no personal knowledge of the events being described in the statement. Frizzy admitted he didn't know what the driver was doing. Only the rear seat passengers could see what was

> going on in the front. Additionally, Judge, this is not a case where the state can impeach their own witness. I say this because Frizzy has not affirmatively damaged their case. He's only disappointed them by leaving out one small but crucial line. Nonetheless, it's not like he's saying he knows the defendant didn't do anything wrong."

That's pretty much it.

These facts were actually taken from a real life case. To see what happened in the real case you can find the details at *People v. Blakey*, 2015 IL App (3d) 130719 (November).

But back to our example, the judge tells the attorney,

> "Well, thank you counsel. You have a very well-thought-out argument. I was a bit confused on some of the issues, so I'm glad you laid it out like that, counsel for the state, what do you have to say?"

At this point, the prosecutor is pretty much agreeing with you and kind of knows they don't got much hope for a prior inconsistent statement under the statute. They can see they also likely won't get it in for impeachment purposes either.

Instead, counsel says,

"How about excited utterance, Judge?"

At this point, the judge says he is going to grant the defendant's objection. He tells the prosecutor to ask another question unless he's got a better argument.

You can get an idea from this example why attorneys might choke under pressure. There is a lot to keep organized and keep straight in a very small amount of time.

As we said before, it helps if much of the brain power has been applied well before the trial, especially with recorded statements. Although you don't know for sure what a witness will say, flagging the witnesses with recorded statements before trial may have given counsel a leg up on being ready to quickly and accurately react during the trial.

This example gives you a good idea of what needs to be going through your head when this issue comes up.

In the final chapter you'll see an organized framework for organizing these thoughts. You'll also get a chance to download a helpful checklist on impeachment and prior inconsistent statements.

10

The Checklist Bringing It All Together

We started this book by talking about impeachment-only evidence. That's where it all began. The current statute and evidentiary rule on prior inconsistent statements as substantive evidence were built right on top of the classical impeachment paradigm.

Both classical impeachment and the current prior inconsistent statement depend on the same foundational questions to execute. Even though it made a lot of sense to discuss classical impeachment before prior inconsistent statements, now it's time to "flip" our thinking.

What we need now is an overarching, analytical way to organize our thinking when questions on impeachment and prior inconsistent statements come up.

When you begin to think about a question that comes up at trial you should first "rule in" or "rule out" the application of the statute.

First you should ask if the prior statement under investigation meets the elements of 725 ILCS 5/115-10.1. After you consider the statute you may find you don't need any further analysis. If there is more analysis required, then you move on to the impeachment question.

It's better to be clear in your head which statements are consistent with the statute. This way if a witness veers off course you know you'll be proceeding under 725 ILCS 5/115-10.1.

This is better because if you can impeach an individual with a prior inconsistent statement under the statute, you're always going to want to do that over classical impeachment.

If you can, it's always better to argue an issue substantively. At closing argument substantive evidence is always better than impeachment-only testimony. This distinction is crucial in many cases. It's everything in other cases.

Once you're clear in your head if you're proceeding under the statute, a lot of the problems and a lot of the concerns associated with classical impeachment simply dissolve away.

For instance, once you know you are proceeding under the statute, the affirmative damage rule doesn't apply anymore. You don't have to go and get hung up on that if you don't need to. If you know you are getting into a prior inconsistent statement consistent with 725 ILCS 5/115-10.1 then who cares if the other side is affirmatively damaged? Doesn't matter.

When you know you are proceeding under the statue everything will be much easier. There's no stress about what to do if the witness flips. There's no anxiety about whether the witness will admit the statement or not admit it. Doesn't matter.

You know exactly what you'll do next if a witness flips on you.

Therefore, in a trial an attorney should first be focused on determining if the prior inconsistent statement can be proven substantively. They need to start there and this will streamline the thinking in a trial.

When a prior inconsistent statement issue comes up at trial, the analysis of the questions that run through the lawyer's head should look like this:

1) First consider the threshold issues. This is when the internal alarm bells begin to vibrate.

- Ask if the statement is truly inconsistent? Most times this is a no-brainer. Other times this could be a legitimate question.
- Second, the lawyer should determine if the inconsistent statement is material and non-collateral. Is it worth the fuss to make a stink about it? Usually it's pretty obvious when you have a material inconsistency but you can't impeach a witness on collateral (insignificant) matters.
- Are you sure the witness is available for cross-examination? If the witness is in court you won't have a problem here. However, be on red alert for witnesses who are claiming a privilege or who are so emotionally distraught on the bench that they can't put words together. There is an argument

that this kind of witness is not available for cross.

2) Next thing is to determine if we are dealing with a substantive prior inconsistent statement that meets the elements of the statute.

- Ask if the prior inconsistent statement has been sworn to in a prior trial, hearing or proceeding?
- Do you have transcripts on this witness from an earlier trial?
- Did the witness make a statement before the grand jury?
- This is how you should be thinking about the issue. If you know you got paper on the witness from a trial, hearing, or previous proceeding, **you know you have a statement under the statute**.

3) If, on the other hand, you don't have transcripts from a prior trial, hearing, or proceeding, then you have to ask if the witness made a recorded, written, or acknowledged statement.

- Do you have a video recording of the witness talking?
- Do you have a digital recording of the interview?
- Is there a written statement or a signed statement?
- Did you or the other side run a full-blown acknowledgment hearing with the witness before trial?

4) Does the witness have personal knowledge?
- If you know you have a statement as described in #3 above, you've got to confirm that the witness had personal knowledge of the thing that was talked about.
- Make sure the witness was there and saw the deed and just didn't hear about it from someone else.

- If you know the witness has personal knowledge of the information recorded, written down, or acknowledged, then you're good. **You know you have a prior inconsistent statement** under 725 ILCS 5/115-10.1.

5) If you can't meet the elements of the statute, the game is not over. Ask: Can I get into the prior statement for impeachment purposes only? You still need to determine if the witness can be impeached under the classical system.

- Does good-old-fashion impeachment apply? You take what you can get. If it does apply you have to be careful to only attack the witness's credibility, and you can't argue the information substantively as evidence.
- To make sure you can proceed under classical impeachment, remember to check who's calling the witness? **The side that is on cross-examination can always impeach the witness.**
- Did the witness cause any affirmative damage to the side that called the witness? If it's their witness did the witness really say something that put the other side in worse shape? If it's your witness you have to critically ask if the witness has hurt your case? Witnesses who say they forgot or can't remember aren't affirmatively hurting the party. If there is **no affirmative damage to the side calling the witness there can be no impeachment.**

6) Finally, before you turn your brain off, ask yourself if everyone (including yourself) is following all the foundational requirements accurately.

- Are the questions being asked the right way in the correct

form?
- Are the three C's being diligently followed?
- Are the parties ready and able to perfect their impeachment with the necessary impeachment witnesses?

This is generally how an attorney should think through the process when this issue first arises in a trial.

On the final pages I put together some resources for you. You'll find a checklist that summarizes the main analytical points you'll want to cover when an impeachment or prior inconsistent statement problem presents itself.

It's something you can refer to during trial prep. If you are in a jam in the middle of a trial, a quick peek might get you out of some trouble. I also put together a list of other materials and resources you may want to read or listen to for more information on this topic.

Well, that is all for now. The goal is for you to not fumble the next prior inconsistent statement problem that presents itself. A little thinking about the rules, what they mean, and thinking about the exact scenarios you could see go a long way. In no time impeachment with a prior inconsistent statement will become automatic for you.

About the Author

Samuel Partida, Jr. podcasts on the Illinois criminal law. He captures the most valuable nuggets from the cases and reports his findings in audio format. You can listen to the Criminal Nuggets Podcast totally free. If you prefer a more rigorous following of the case law consider subscribing to the Premium Nuggets Podcast. Go here to learn more:

IllinoisCaseLaw.com

CriminalNuggets.com

PremiumNuggets.com

partidasam@IllinoisCaselaw.com

Impeachment & Prior Inconsistent Statement Cheat Sheet

Threshold Questions
- [ ] Is It Inconsistent?
- [ ] Is It Material?
- [ ] Subject To Cross?

Prior Inconsistent Statement Analysis
- [ ] Sworn To Under Oath
    - [ ] Trial?
    - [ ] Hearing?
    - [ ] Grand Jury?
    - [ ] Other Proceeding?
    - [ ] If YES - It's substance proceed with foundation questions
    - [ ] If NO proceed below
- [ ] Not Sworn To Under Oath
    - [ ] Recorded?
    - [ ] Written?
    - [ ] Signed?
    - [ ] Acknowledged?
    - [ ] If YES - It could be substantive proceed to question below
    - [ ] If NO - It's not substantive proceed to impeachment analysis
- [ ] Personal Knowledge
    - [ ] If YES - It's substance proceed with foundation questions
    - [ ] If NO - It's not substantive proceed to impeachment only analysis

Impeachment Analysis
- [ ] Cross-Examining Side CAN Impeach
- [ ] Side Calling The Witness
    - [ ] If NO Affirmative Damage CAN'T impeach
    - [ ] If YES Affirmative Damage CAN impeach

Foundation - The 3 C's
- [ ] Commit
- [ ] Confirm (Time, Date, Location, Circumstances)
- [ ] Confront
- [ ] Impeaching Witness Ready To Perfect?

Additional Resources

The 3 Best Cases To Read

❶ *People v. Brothers*, 2015 IL App (4th) 130644 (September)

❷ *People v. Lewis*, 2017 IL App (4th) 150124 (April)

❸ *People v. Evans*, 2016 IL App (3d) 140120 (July)

---

2 Awesome Free Audio Recordings

❶ IllinoisCaseLaw.com/Steigmann

❷ IllinoisCaseLaw.com/Meyers

Download All Of The Above AND...

❶ **The Checklist Cheat Sheet**
❷ **Plus Even More Resources**

Go Here To Get It All:

IllinoisCaseLaw.com/more-statements